ADVENTURES IN MANIFESTING

ADVENTURES IN MANIFESTING

HEALING FROM WITHIN

Sarah Prout and Sean Patrick Simpson

The Adventures In Manifesting series: Volume #4.
First published 2012 by Älska Publishing

Office based in Melbourne, Australia

Typeset in Giovanni LT 9/12/14 pt

© Sarah Prout and Sean Patrick Simpson

The moral rights of the authors have been asserted.

National Library of Australia Cataloguing-in-Publishing entry:

Authors:	Prout, Sarah 1979 – / Simpson, Sean Patrick 1984 –
Title:	Adventures In Manifesting: Healing from Within
ISBN:	9780987325921 (pbk) 9780987325945 (ebook)
Subjects:	Self help, New Age Publications, Inspiration
Dewey Number:	158.1

Cover design by Sarah Prout

Editorial revisions in house

Printed in Hong Kong

Also available in electronic format

*note that grammar and US/UK English is sometimes reflected in each author's preferred writing style.

www.AlskaPublishing.com

Wholesale Discounts
For competitive rates on bulk purchases, please go to www.AlskaPublishing.com

Disclaimer
The material in this publication is of the nature of general comment only and does not represent professional advice. To the maximum extent permitted by the law, the authors and publisher disclaim all responsibility and liability to any person, arising directly or indirectly from any person taking or not taking action based upon the information in this publication.

Älska means to LOVE

(Say it like this: *elsh-ka*)

This book is lovingly dedicated to your heart and the well-being of your life's adventure.

CONTENTS

GRATITUDE

With the deepest gratitude we would like to thank all of the Älska authors for sharing their incredible and inspiring stories in this book. We would also like to thank our students in the **AdventuresInManifesting.org** community and *you* (the reader) for supporting the Älska vision of Love and Oneness.

From Sean:

The creation of the latest three Adventures in Manifesting books have been an absolutely incredible and inspiring process. My deepest gratitude is with our project manager Mark Rhapsody for all he has done.

To Sarah Prout– you are amazing and I love you. It is such a joy waking up to you each morning and spending our days playing in the fields of Älska Publishing. Living in the now, reminiscing on the past and dreaming about the future with you is amazing.

To Amr and Angel – thank you for your incredible work. To Olivia and Thomas who are a constant reminder to *be the change*. S&D – You're always to be thanked. To Mom and Dad, you guys rock. To Cody, my crew, friends at Mt. SAC, Mr. Rogers, Mr. Mac, and Pro – I might not have been here to write my story had it not been for you. Thank you for everything we have shared and the inspiration *you* have all given me.

To some of my greatest inspirations I have yet to meet and befriend: Oprah, Ellen, Will Smith, Jim Carrey, and Richard Branson. Thank you for *being* and inspiring the world not just through what you do, but by who you are.

To everyone in my life, my deepest love and gratitude is with you.

From Sarah:

I would like to thank my dad (Mr. A.A Prout) for your love and support. Your kindness and help with the kids is so greatly appreciated – I love you.

To my man, Mr. Sean Patrick Simpson – you're my best friend and I adore you. Your sublime management skills and dedication to the rapid growth of our company and vision is a true inspiration.

Thomas and Olivia, I love you with all my heart. Thank you for being the beautiful souls that you are.

To my friends, family, and soul family (you know who you are) – thanks for your amazing love and support. It means the world to me.

Many thanks to our awesome team behind the scenes here at Älska-Publishing that keep the company running like a well-oiled machine.

Last but not least… our fur babies Cookie LaLa and Merlin Moon-man – you really are amazing little souls in dog suits.

INTRODUCTION

Älska

It is with soul-felt gratitude that we would like to welcome you to the *Adventures in Manifesting* series. It has been designed as a source you will continuously enjoy reading when in search of insight, wisdom, and inspiration. The stories are shared from people just like you that are on a wondrous journey of self-discovery.

From a multitude of unique vantage points, these stories demonstrate active examples of inner guidance, connection, faith, and love that have transcended all limitations. Each story has been written with you in mind.

Reading with Your Soul

Our advice to you is that you read with an open heart, an open mind, and absorb the information that sparks your own adventure in manifesting. When reading from a place of wonderment and curiosity, you are bound to find deep resonance. Ask yourself, "What here resonates with me? What inspired action am I being guided to take? What can I learn from this now?"

Allow yourself to find a connection point within each story and within yourself that is right for you.

Your Own Treasure Map

While you will discover truths that each author has found for themselves, you can find in-between the lines your own truths as well. The wonder of this book is that understanding and resonating with certain concepts will happen at different points in your life. So take your time. Keep the book by your bedside table. Pick it up when you feel inspired and follow your inner guidance to the story you're meant to draw from now. Whether you read through it all in one sitting, or piece-by-piece, you will find this a place of inspiration for years to come.

The Mission of Älska

The mission of Älska is to bestow the teachings of love and oneness and proliferate its message throughout the world. Within these two illuminated concepts is the power of vibrancy, creativity, joy, and inspiration. While the mechanisms of metaphysical principles here have been in place since the dawn of time, it is our purest intention to continue this work that began to gain prominence at the beginning of the 19th century in the New Thought Movement.

What are you Manifesting?

You may have noticed on the front cover this very powerful question. Ask yourself this to begin reading with some basic intentions and ideas of what you desire. Just as we would teach you, we are *acting as if* and actively demonstrating how to imprint the Universe with the vibration of success, thus the questions.

In the years before Jim Carrey became a superstar, he wrote himself a check for $10 million dollars and added "for acting services rendered". He carried it in his wallet from that day forth until the abundance and recognition that he desired started to manifest in his life. This act of setting an almighty intention contributed to his success eventually growing to fruition. As witnessed, the Universe responds to what is radiated energetically.

Your Journey Begins Now

Start it from a place of love and gratitude, knowing that as you read you will find resonance with what you are in alignment with in this point of time.

You will find yourself beginning to develop a story through direct experience of your intended reality. As you do, we will be here waiting with expectant joy and an open heart to see what you have to share with the world as well.

Until then, we will look forward to hearing all about your own adventures in manifesting.

With Love and Gratitude,
Älska

About Älska

Älska is the combined energies of Sarah Prout and Sean Patrick Simpson. The company name means *Love* and was received as gentle guidance one evening after a very intense session of laughter and joy.

You say it like this: 'elsh-ka' – which is slightly different than the original Scandinavian pronunciation of their verb (which means *to love*).

Sean and Sarah were prompted from within to start a metaphysical publishing company based on their mutual adoration of Universal truth and passion for writing. Hence, Älska was created!

http://www.alskapublishing.com

THE MANIFESTING COURSE

Get The Manifesting Course and join the Adventures in Manifesting community to connect with other like-minded and inspired individuals:

www.AdventuresInManifesting.org

Share Your Experience

Has a particular story, insight or teaching stood out to you?

We'd love to hear about your experience, so feel free to get in touch and let us know. You can e-mail us at:

feedback@adventuresinmanifesting.org

Additionally, with the intention and desire to share stories and teachings from all walks of life, we'd like to invite you to potentially be a part of one of the next *Adventures in Manifesting* titles.

Stories of all topics about manifesting are welcome (success, spirituality, health, happiness, wealth, love, prosperity, inner guidance, achieving dreams, overcoming obstacles, etc.)

If chosen as a top submission, we will get in touch directly to invite you to be a part of one of our next *Adventures in Manifesting* titles.

Please go to www.AdventuresInManifesting.org to share your experience (not to mention join the course and community, as well as find the hard copy, Kindle and iBook versions of other titles in the series).

Enjoy!

DEAR UNIVERSE, GIVE ME STRENGTH

Sarah Prout

The day I got married back in April 2001, I was just twenty-one years old, four months pregnant, and had a massive bruise on my arm from where my husband-to-be had beaten me only weeks earlier. I was wearing a flowing pale blue dress with my little belly sticking out. I tried my very best to cover the bruise – that spanned from my shoulder to elbow – with make-up, but it was an unsuccessful attempt.

Surrounded by friends, family, and flowers, it was truly beautiful, but I felt like we were building a house on sand. The marriage was an act of sheer denial; a choice that would unfold a vicious ten-year cycle where my soul would pay the ultimate price until I was ready to face the truth.

Sometimes I'm so mad at myself that I choose to hide and protect him rather than making him accountable for his actions. *I should have called the police. I should have told my parents. I should have had the courage to stand up for me and my unborn child.*

During our marriage there was love. I really loved him so much, but the flipside of that coin was the extreme opposite.

Like all abusive relationships, it's hard to see when you are part of the cycle of pain. Sometimes things are going really well for a while and you convince yourself that you're in the right place and doing the best thing for the family. Then the violence and neglect peeks into the situation again and again making you question yourself.

My healing process from this abuse has been complicated and arduous to say the very least.

What I was looking for was *safety*. My lack of self-love and bravery left me feeling empty. I was on a constant quest for an exit strategy.

I remember that on New Year's Eve in 2008 I was sitting on the steps in my garden all alone. I could hear fireworks off in the distance and people cheering. At my house, the children were asleep and my husband snapped at me for choosing a movie he didn't enjoy, so he went to bed early. I sat outside listening to classical music and stared up at the stars feeling so alone. I pleaded with the Universe to get me out of this situation and to give me strength. Loneliness is like decay for the soul. When you're a vibrant person that loves to laugh, talk, and be heard, it really dims your shine to be alone.

I finally left in the New Year.

I was weak. I fell in love with the first person that showed me affection and I had an affair. However, it was not intentional. This person just made me see how rotten my marriage was and offered me a better life. So I left one man for another still seeking safety without truly believing in myself, seeing the situation for what it was.

The guilt and shame of the affair was almost identically parallel to the guilt and shame of being punched by my husband. I had created this maze of pain and the only way to navigate myself out of the situation was to ride it out and trust that my series of bad choices would eventually lead to a good one.

The day I said I was leaving was one I will never forget. I had slept with this other guy once and confessed my actions to my husband in order to clear my conscience. I felt rotten about it and knew that I would burst if I didn't say something sooner rather than later.

My husband seemed fine about it and said, "Well if you didn't have an affair I probably would have." We knew we needed to get some space to think, so I went out for dinner.

When I returned home, I found all of my clothes destroyed, my jewellery smashed to smithereens, and pretty much everything I owned out on the lawn with gasoline poured onto it.

My husband was blind-drunk and walking around the house in his underpants with a hammer in his hand. He had just smashed my MacBook and cut my desk in half with a saw! He was desperately looking for a box of matches to light the mountain of gasoline-doused clothes on fire. Had he succeeded, the house could have gone up in flames.

The saddest part is that I had left him to look after the children. His rampage began without me even knowing they were in danger.

They were huddled up under the covers together, absolutely terrified by what Daddy had been doing. I peeled back the blanket to see two sets of terrified eyes staring at me wondering what on earth was going on.

It was 3 a.m. The only thing to do was call the police. My husband was angry and I was in danger. For the first time ever, I knew I needed to break the cycle and set myself free once and for all.

All I remember is that when the police arrested him, I was rushing around to find him a pair of socks so his feet wouldn't get cold. Even in the midst of the destruction, I was still feeling love and compassion towards him.

I was so calm and non-reactive even though the only clothes I owned were the ones I was wearing. All of my worldly possessions were now gone and yet inwardly I felt like this was the first time in my life I was standing up for myself. The only moment I broke down was when the police officer asked me the names and birthdates of my beautiful children.

Long story short, I moved in with the man I had an affair with and discovered that there was no way in the world it would work out. It was such a lightning-fast romance that I left after only eight weeks and moved states to live with my mother for a while.

And can you guess what happened next?

Three months passed and I moved back in with my husband.

I know. You must be thinking I'm crazy, right?

Sticks and Stones

I'm not sure why I moved back in to partake in the dysfunction again. Looking back, I really do question my sanity. I guess having no money, no security, and two children is pretty terrifying.

My husband and I were living in the same house in different beds with an intervention order in place until I could save enough money to get my own little apartment in Melbourne.

Time and time again he overstepped the terms of the intervention order, screaming, yelling, and threatening to hurt me. Too often my foot wedged in front of a door to keep him out of my room.

Whore. Bitch. Slut. Ugly, old slapper.

My children heard me being called these names.

On a Friday, I decided to move states again to keep my children safe. On the Monday I had made $12,000 by launching an online product at the same time I landed my contract to write my book, *The Power of Influence*.

The Universe rewarded me because I made a firm decision to move on.

When you surrender and you are clear about what you wish to attract, then you manifest your desires a lot faster. I discuss this theme a lot more in depth in The Manifesting Course at the *Adventures in Manifesting* community.

Beginning to Love Myself

I left and didn't look back.

The transition process during a divorce is one you can only really understand if you have been through it yourself. It's ugly, it's messy, and it's really painful. But I think the courage required to follow your heart and finally break away is worth every single tincture of heartache, especially if you're in an abusive relationship.

In 2010, I finally got divorced. Ten years of marriage didn't end in a big *ka-ching* for me. Single motherhood hoisted me into the greatest heights of self-empowerment. I had no clue how I was going to support myself. I left my marriage with over $30,000 of debt. I was on the single mother's pension, running my business from home, and struggling with cash-flow to support myself and two children after moving from Melbourne to Noosa, Australia.

At times, I felt like a failure.

My life no longer appeared as the *normal* (whatever that is) façade of family life. You know, the one with the doting and attentive mother at home, the daddy at work and the kids being washed, fed, and entertained like clockwork. I felt so ashamed of the violence, aggression, and neglect my children had endured.

Trust me, I had my fair share of crying fits, wondering whether I'd done the right thing and desperately seeking the safety of being taken care of... but there was no one. I had to learn to suck it up and *be my own security for the first time ever.*

The dark times were nasty. I mean, *really* nasty. I went from my super-comfortable life in Melbourne to not having a washing machine for six months! I tell you, when you have two children then you *need* a washing machine! My mother gave me the best advice ever, and that was to take everything one day at a time. *It's all about where you choose to place your focus.*

I literally had to create my life again from scratch; all new furniture, my own car, my own freedom, my own space. It was awesome! I chose to turn my cloud into a whole skyline of clouds with a silver lining. And when I chose to take responsibility for myself, my life started to change for the better.

When I started to heal, my true love arrived.

I wasn't looking for love but I found Sean Patrick Simpson. We met online back in 2009 and I confided in him about all of the violence and emotional upheaval that I was experiencing.

Something sparked and we fell in love back in mid-2010.

I truly believe that if I hadn't been through a violent, shitty relationship for a decade, I couldn't have attracted such a wonderful man that is everything to me. He's amazing with my kids, he's my best friend, and I love him with all of my heart.

The healing from within is one that I am blessed to experience hand-in-hand with my life-partner, Sean. There's no safety or approval seeking. Our relationship just flows and is in alignment with the desires of my heart.

I get letters and emails from women (and some men) all over the world that have read about my story. One woman in particular told me that hearing about my journey gave her the courage to speak up about her own violent relationship. I truly believe that the power of storytelling has the miraculous essence to change lives, which is why we created the *Adventures in Manifesting* series.

The best piece of advice I could give you?

Love you first. *Always.*

About the Author

Sarah Prout is the co-founder of Älska Publishing, the *Adventures in Manifesting* series, and award-winning entrepreneur. Her bestselling book *The Power of Influence* has been sold internationally and translated for European distribution.

Sarah's love for metaphysics, design, and business empowerment shines through in her writing, artwork, and teachings. Since 2006, Sarah has built an impressive international media and client portfolio inspiring people to create their own reality.

She reaches over 55,000 followers in over twenty-four countries around the globe with heartfelt, vibrant, and empowering advice about love, business, and style.

http://www.adventuresinmanifesting.org

http://www.sarahprout.com

BLEEDING FROM THE HEART

Sean Patrick Simpson

Blood dripped down my fingers. On my knees, my left hand gripped the knife tightly, my right hand awaiting another slice.

With tears streaming down my face, I took another slice. And another. And another.

More blood. Cuts covered both sides of my hand; some on my arm. The pain was searing. But it was not the cuts that hurt. It was my heart. My soul.

Is this it? Is this what it comes down to? Am I ready to kill myself? No, I'm not ready. But if not now, when? I can't go on much longer feeling this way…

I found myself next at my parents' bedroom door. "Mom," I cried, "can you come here?"

She knew something was terribly wrong. As she got her robe, I defeatedly walked back to my bedroom.

Back on my knees with the knife sitting beside me and with blood splotches on the white carpet, I sat in blood and tears. My head down in heartless defeat, my mom walked in to witness her worst nightmare.

Her son was considering killing himself.

Attached

Between eighteen and twenty years of age, it was from loving with all my heart, to rejection and heartbreak, then to depression and despair, that lead me to this terrible experience.

Nearing the end of high school I had my first love. Filled with dreams of the future and the love we would share, I believed we were meant to be.

This was also the first time this kind of love was so quickly ended, leaving me rejected, depressed, and feeling like my whole world had shattered – like nothing else mattered. At the start of college, crying the entire forty-five-minute drive to school, as well as mourning in my car between classes, became a daily ritual.

I was a mess.

Just months after starting college and in the midst of this depression, I fell for another woman who was just as lost as I was. Two people drowning however cannot save one another, and that too ended terribly. When it did, I lost eleven pounds in a week, and over the months I became so sick that just receiving a phone call from her would make me throw up.

Soon after, the pain got so bad that I would gaze at the kitchen knives as I walked past. I had never understood why someone would ever cut themselves. Yet during that time, it seemed as though I craved it. I wanted to know what it was like.

Darkness followed me everywhere. It became my constant companion.

What in the world could possibly have made me so *attached* that, when rejected, I was left depressed for months on end while the other person moved on? What could have made me so *dependent* on the love of another that I constantly imagined ending my life and came to believe I would not see the age of twenty-five?

Crashing the car, a gun to the temple, a bottle of pills… they were all considerations. All possibilities.

The knife was my first experiment. And, fortunately, my last.

Where it All Began

They say the Universe throws back at you over and over again the experiences from which lessons you have not yet learned. Clearly, I was not learning my own.

I wonder thinking back where exactly the patterns of depression and attachment began. Considering we are the creators of our own reality, surely I was somehow attracting the experience. After all, the cycle of love and rejection was not a rare occurrence for me. It continued for years after my cutting, and I believe initially began many, *many* years before.

From an early age, I was getting crushes on girls one after another, believing in my heart that each of them was *the one*. The depth of pain I would feel when the love wasn't reciprocated though was unfathomable. This wasn't just experienced with the desire of a significant other though. With all relationships, I had unbearably strong *attachments*. And so, I manifested the feelings of *lack* that came with that neediness.

The Universe always works as a mirror to reflect back to you the energy that you send out there.

It's not that I was a particularly unhappy person. On the contrary, I was incredibly happy, with a loving and supportive family environment. My closest friends would even describe me over the years as a passionate and positive being. It's just that my emotions were *extreme* on both ends of the spectrum. I could get really high on excitement and love, yet get critically low on depression and sadness.

With each high there tended to be an even deeper low until I navigated my way back to safety.

Taking The Burden

For each friendship I did create, whether maintained or not, I loved *hard!* In my heart and mind they were the moon and the stars. They were mine to look after and care for: my family; my soul connections; my life.

Along with these feelings and beliefs came a deep burden I was ready and eager to bear: to *always* put them first. To *always* put their needs before my own. To *always* love them unconditionally, no matter what. If I developed a friendship, then I had taken a vow of commitment. And this is exactly what I created for myself: a constant life experience where my own needs came *second*.

I was essentially the most loyal friend a person could have. If ever they needed me, I would drop everything to be there for them, *no matter what.*

Little did I realize just how damaging this mindset could be to my own life.

As I said, in every way, I loved *hard.*

Putting Myself First

In looking back, the lessons I needed to learn are clear to see. The primary one: To *love with non-attachment.* The unobvious one though was to create a life in which *I am whole within* as well as putting myself *first.*

There was nothing wrong with the vow to always love my friends unconditionally. And the idea of always putting them and their own needs before my own was a noble one. However, there was a fundamental flaw in my twisted understanding of what *always putting them first* actually meant...

And that was not *always* looking out for me as well.

Looking out for me didn't necessarily mean I had to drop the ball on those I cared for. But the thing is, I had the specific mindset of, *I will carry the weight of the world and put myself through hell if it means being there for a friend.* With these thoughts, it's no surprise I manifested and created that exact experience for myself: with pain so unbearable that I considered taking my own life.

Loving Yourself So Much That Nothing Else Matters

It's important to realize throughout our journey that we do in fact create our own reality, both internally and externally. Focusing on the outer world first though is backwards, and that is exactly what I did over the years. By not focusing on creating wholeness within first, I was instead obsessed with experiences embodying *lack* when those people and things I attached to could not stay in my life the way I wanted.

When a person focuses inwardly and manifests wholeness, they create a space filled with so much love that happiness is no longer dependent on what happens, who does this or that, or what type of feelings are reciprocated. Instead, happiness becomes the person's way of *being*, regardless of what's happening around them. No longer dependent on the love of another, you are fully *independent* through the love you create for yourself.

This independence is exactly what I needed to learn and manifest to come to that place of wholeness.

How it Came to Pass

Another way to look at being whole is to embrace *self-love*.

Had this idea of self-love been suggested to me during those years of emotional extremes, I'm not so sure I would have heard or accepted it. In fact, I might have even thought it to be a ridiculous and self-indulgent notion.

If we are not whole ourselves though, how then could we ever expect to *give our all* to others? How could we ever expect to be capable of giving the purest of love when we have not created the pureness within? Self sacrifice of one's happiness to provide for another *is not* sustainable. When we realize this and *choose to create love* within ourselves, we have so much more to give.

As the creators of our own reality, the love we experience is not up to others; it is up to us.

You must love yourself first; not last. You must look out for *you*. You must care for *you*. You must love… *you*.

The Evolving Experience of Letting Go

Over the years, another great lesson I learned was *acceptance and surrender*. This meant maintaining my intentions and desires, but embracing my every experience and *being okay with whatever happened*. Had I found the ability to do this years before, combined with self-love, I would have saved myself from a lot of heartache and been much more at peace.

As I had mentioned, the Universe will throw back at you the experiences from which lessons you have not yet learned. And on this level of non-attachment, I had another to learn...

Three and a half years ago I met my love, Sarah Prout.

We met online via Twitter and instantly became friends. Little did we know that we would soon become so much more. And a year later, we found ourselves together kissing on the beaches of Australia, madly in love.

There was just one problem: I was attached to my life in America. My dreams for the future, my friendships, my family... they were all there. Having lived on opposite sides of the world, one of us would have had to leave our current life behind. Considering she had two kids aged four and nine, this naturally had to be me.

Eventually, after quite the inner struggle, I made the decision to be with my love – or to at least take the first step in that direction.

Yet still, even as I got on the plane to come back to Australia, I was torn. I wanted so strongly to be with Sarah, but I felt like I was having to give up everything else I knew and loved.

It was finally time for me to truly get this art of acceptance and surrender; to embrace the experience fully and completely no matter what the ultimate decision was to be (to stay or to go back to America).

And so I took that first step towards creating a new life.

Affirmation to Manifest Wholeness

Letting go of all that I clung to was not easy. My attachments still remained strong. And for some time I felt like I was *giving up* a part of me. But this decision was something I needed to do to learn the lessons the Universe kept trying to teach me: to finally *create* wholeness within, where I could truly embrace life with non-attachment, filled with both love for others *and* myself.

And that's exactly the place I came to.

Once I was there, I realized nothing was ever truly given up. Life was simply transformed. I still had my friends. I still had my home in America to go back to and visit. But rather than being in a space of lack where I missed and *longed* for those people and experiences, I *looked forward* to them.

All those years I thought I was at a loss when people would stray from my life, it turns out, I never lacked anything. It was simply a reality that I created for myself by embracing *the idea* of pain and lack of wholeness. Now, I embrace a new reality in which I can be, have and do anything I wish.

Wholeness is always here and need only be realized to begin manifesting the experience and creating the life we love.

Today, I realize my wholeness.

Now, I live in happiness and joy.

Now, I live in love and gratitude.

Now, I accept, surrender and embrace life as it *is*.

And all it took was that first step.

About the Author

Sean Patrick Simpson is the co-founder of Älska Publishing and co-creator of the *Adventures in Manifesting* series. He writes and speaks on topics such as mindset, metaphysics, spirituality, business and language patterns.

A musician and singer at heart, Sean has had his compositions played for over 31 million people internationally. You can connect with him and the other authors and readers of this book through the Adventures in Manifesting community.

http://www.adventuresinmanifesting.org

http://www.seanpatricksimpson.com

THE SECRET WISDOM OF THE INNER VOICE

Dr. John Demartini

What better way of creating a more fulfilling life than by mastering the art of tuning into your most inspired and ingenious self, your inner voice? This voice is your guide of all guides to a life of greatness. You cannot attune to this inspiring voice without living a more inspiring life. Genius, creativity, and a silent power emerge from your heart and mind the moment you do. The secret of tuning into its magnificent messages is having a heart filled with gratitude.

When your heart is opened wide with gratitude, your inner voice becomes loud and clear, and your most life expanding messages enter into your mind with ease. If your heart is filled with gratitude, it is almost impossible to stop your inner voice from speaking clearly and profoundly. Many great spiritual revelations and mental attributes are suddenly birthed from within you when your voice on the inside becomes louder than the many voices or opinions on the outside.

The immortal masters of life have been those who have mastered the ability to attune to their great inner voices. Those great beings that mastered this talent left their marks in history. From Christ, who listened to his heavenly Father, to Dante, who listened to Beatrice, to Walt Whitman, and many others who listened to their guiding whisper; all have impacted humanity with the resultant immortal expressions of their inner voice.

As your voice on the inside grows in clarity and strength, so will your inspiration when you listen. Begin to attune to that inspiring station from within. Listen as it guides you to new levels of creativity and operation. Your inner voice will put few or no limits on your life. Only the many outer voices of others who allow themselves to live a life of mediocrity will do so. Decide now to expand your wisdom and fulfillment through such careful listening.

Follow the steps below and commune with this wise inner guide. It will help you create a greater contribution to others and possibly even a legacy.

1. Stand relaxed with your hands loosely at your side. Take a few deep breaths. Inhale and exhale through the nose slowly.

2. Tilt your head up 30 degrees.

3. Turn your eyes up another 30 degrees, until you are looking forward and upward.

4. Close your eyelids and let them become relaxed.

5. Think about something or someone you are truly and deeply grateful for.

6. Keep thinking and thanking until you feel your heart has truly opened up and you have even experienced a tear of inspiration.

7. Upon attaining a grateful state, now ask your inner voice for any guiding message. Ask, "Inner voice do you have a message for me at this moment?"

8. When you are grateful enough and you ask for a message a message will clearly come.

9. Write this message down.

10. If your message does not become immediately and clearly revealed, repeat steps 6 – 10 until it does.

When you are truly grateful you will receive amazing and inspiring inner messages. These messages will be more powerful than might at first be apparent. The master, the genius, is the one who listens carefully. When you are grateful and your heart becomes opened, you will have revealed before your mind the inner message you would love to fulfill. These priceless gems of guiding revelation will assist you in living a life of greatness.

Be sure to act on your inspirations as soon as possible. When you don't follow the inspirations and intuitions of your inner voice promptly you can begin to emotionally beat your self up. This is not terrible though for it is simply part of the grand and magnificent design of conscious evolution. It is a blessing for it assures that no matter what happens, you will eventually learn and gradually or immediately unfold your inner spiritual mission, talent, and destiny. Life events will at times force you to listen to that wise voice within. The inspired beings throughout history learned to follow it. Those who have ignored it have passed by many opportunities it could have provided.

For decades many psychologist have considered individuals who have heard their inner voices as bordering on the edge of sanity. But, if you look carefully at the many great spiritual leaders, scientists, artists, musicians, and social leaders, they regularly listened to their inner voices. They gratefully awakened this special inner communion regularly. The great philosophers have stated that they would rather have the whole world against them than their own inner soul. Today, you have an opportunity for expanding your greatness. When your wise and masterful voice on the inside becomes greater than the many little voices on the outside, a life of great fulfillment, wisdom, and genius can become yours.

About the Author

Dr. Demartini is considered one of the world's leading authorities on human behavior and personal development. He is the founder of the Demartini Institute, a private research and education organization with a curriculum of over seventy-two different courses covering multiple aspects of human development.

http://www.drdemartini.com

FACE IT: MIRACLES CAN HAPPEN

Renee Airya

"You are going to die, soon, if you don't find out what is going on with you."

I wake up the next day and write the same words. I listen and question: are these just unstable thoughts? I don't want to die. After this goes on for several days, I decide I have to find out what the truth is. My body pushes me out of the house and into my journey.

Here I am, in my late twenties, a fitness model and healer, visiting doctors, when just a few months ago I was posing for a swimsuit calendar in Hawaii. This is all very bizarre for me. Although I get messages that I *am* going to die, the doctors proclaim that I look like the picture of health and that all of my tests are *normal*.

No definitive answers. No conclusions.

I look in the mirror and notice something different, but can't tell what it is. Something has changed. I feel it in my soul.

My head hurts. The right side of my body feels like it is working at 50%. At this point, I am seeing many doctors. "She is a hypochondriac," they say. I am nauseous and I cry for help to a trusted chiropractor. He wants to send me to one last clinic. This is tiring, but I agree to go.

Fast forward three days and one scan later, in a gorgeous California afternoon, I am on my way to get my results. I have a feeling that today is the day and think that I am ready when I am not.

I get there and see my brain scan on the light machine and I instantly feel faint. My reality collapses. I have no idea what is before me, but I fear the best might be behind me. This does not look good.

"Renee, you have a large brain tumor. It is very rare, 10 out of 1 million, and yours is the largest one that I have seen. It is attached to your brainstem and is distorting it. It is a miracle that your symptoms are not worse than they are. Maybe through your healing work, your body re-programmed to be without symptoms, but now you have to get this treated immediately. I am referring you to a brain surgeon."

Well, that would explain it. I am not sure if I can walk back to my car, but at least I know that I am not crazy.

That was the beginning of my brain tumor experience. And from there, I embarked on an even deeper journey into the essence of being a human being. Thankfully, for what I believe was my *sexy intuition* in action, I developed a deep passion for physical and spiritual health about nine years prior to this crisis. I attended every health seminar, meditation event, and certification program that I could and traveled to other states for coaching and healing with the best alternative thinkers and practitioners. And through this education, I developed an understanding of how energy works within the body.

Anyway, back to my story. A part of me was not even afraid of death and I did not even know if I wanted treatment because, after all, my body was choosing this. I talked to a healer who told me that if I had surgery, it would bring immense change because it was my path to be a leader. That sounded right and I knew that my body was not going to heal itself on this one so, by now, this intuition seemed to have a good track record.

So, I met with a *renowned* brain surgeon to whom I was referred. From our first handshake, I did not get a good feeling. As it was, during this upcoming procedure, I would permanently lose hearing on my right side and also lose the balance nerve on the right side. There were severe risks with the other cranial nerves. I wanted to trust this man but I did not.

His office had me apply for state-funding because the surgery was $240,000 and I should qualify because I was considered an emergency life threatening situation and had no health insurance.

I got online and researched surgeon options while questioning how this could be happening to me. I was a nice, loving person and I was only twenty-nine. I eventually found the names of the most successful surgeons, and prayed that somehow, someway, they would find me.

Then, something interesting happened when I went back to the renowned brain surgeon. He introduced me to his *assistant*. And *he* was none other than one of the surgeons I had prayed for the day before! A big, radiant smile lit up my face.

I still did not know how this was all going to come together, yet I felt a magical trust. The following day, I was rushed to the ER because of severe vision problems and vomiting. I was seeing only geometric shapes. The pressure in my head was quickly increasing.

Two days before my surgery, I went in for the pre-surgery check. The surgeon's nurse gave me the news that the doctor had canceled and passed my case to someone who had never even done this procedure before. This was the strangest thing. *What?!* I felt very nervous, but realized that my gut instinct had been right about him from the beginning. Maybe this was Divine intervention?

I called my assistant surgeon and told him what had happened. We were in a real-life time crunch and I prayed. He called back and said that he had arranged for us to work with another top surgeon and when I asked him who that was, to my amazement, he said the name of the other surgeon that I had found online. Now they were *both* on my team!

He also told me that they had compassion for the true urgency of the situation and, due to the emergency state aid not being approved yet, they would perform the surgery free of their charges. They told me, however, I would have to come up with around $40,000 to cover the minimum hospital stay. This was a prayer-answered miracle!

My parents refinanced and pulled together the money and I called together kindred spirits to bless me. This was a stressful, scary, and sacred time.

On the day of my surgery, I had my hair braided down the side where it would be shaved, and a sharpie drawn line on my abdomen that read *put sexy scar here* (for the incision where fat had to be removed and put into my head around a metal plate). I gave gemstones to the staff that would be tending me. Feeling so peaceful, I was so brave going in.

And I surrendered.

When I awakened ten hours later, the only thing I heard was my friend saying, "Something went very wrong."

I was in and out of consciousness after that for two days in the ICU and was vomiting constantly. When I finally arrived into my regular hospital room, I realized that indeed something had gone wrong. I had a plastic patch over my right eye. My vision was blurry and I was about to be confronted with my biggest fear.

My surgeon entered the room. He had tears in his eyes and told me the good news was that the tumor was 100% gone, but the bad news was that my face was paralyzed on the right side because my facial nerve had been severed in order to remove all of the tumor. He explained that my face, including my eye, were unable to move at all on the right side. He suggested that I immediately get a spring put into my eye so that it would blink and close again.

I cried, and felt what it was like to cry only with one eye. Oh, no, I loved my big smile. I asked to look in a mirror and when I did, I did not recognize myself. I was angry and sad. I was so in touch with my humanity and a power welled up inside of me.

Like a rainbow bursting out of a storm, I boldly said, "I will smile and I will sing." It did not seem realistic, but that was my response. I told him that I would heal in six months. He said that it was scientifically impossible.

I stated again that no matter what, I was going to heal my face. One doctor looked at me and said, "Well, she is fired up so that is a good sign!" I also opted out of getting another surgery to protect and fix my eye. It was a dangerous choice but I could not bear another surgery.

So, I went upon my healing journey. I did not eat hospital food, but instead organic greens and essential fatty acids for my brain. I struggled with re-learning coordination to walk again. Watching many other *success* cases go home, I asked God to release my disappointment as I realized I was in for a *very* long recovery process.

The next several months were an incredible witnessing of the power of the human spirit, the Law of Attraction, faith, and dedication.

First, I went to a temporary rental for a month with my mom to recuperate. Then, I slept on friends' sofas because I could not afford rent. I really needed money to pay my bills and for therapy but, obviously, I could not work.

Just in time, my community stepped up and threw a fundraiser, which enabled me to get some necessities. I also found out that the state-funding that never came through pre-surgery was due to someone sending a fax to the wrong person. So, with my eye patch on, and still in recovery, I showed up in court as my own attorney and won repayment! It was a huge but exhausting victory.

Then, more good news came. My friend told me her father had a fundraising opportunity. Since I still needed about $57,000, I visualized this amount coming to me and how exactly I would distribute the funds. She spoke at his event on my behalf and then called with the news that just over $57,000 was raised.

Amazing! I truly saw The Law of Attraction in motion.

My healing process continued on and it was grueling at times. I stood in front of the mirror, daily, focusing on one area of my face and willing it to move. It literally would hurt in my brain because I was so focused. I made myself *be* social, even though it was embarrassing with the eye patch and drooling down one side. Ironically, someone even called me a pirate at the same store that another person had told me (before surgery) that I had one of the most beautiful smiles they had ever seen.

I grieved for my past, but looked to the future. I affirmed my health long before I could physically see it. I envisioned myself hiking in Yosemite and flying around the world, manufacturing a smile in my head all along. Months after surgery, in front of the mirror, I finally felt something. It was the beginning of electricity. I don't even know if I imagined it, but I let myself feel its reality. My face started taking form again. Within a month, I had a smile line that had formed.

My face... was no longer drooping!

I celebrated and created artwork with lots of colors and life. I went to the ocean daily, played in the sand, and did my own intuitive form of physical therapy. I lived in my own studio where I created a safe and loving environment to make my new dreams come true. I followed my heart, took a trip to Europe so I could get lost in art and feel inspired again, and also revisited Hawaii, where I hiked and reclaimed my past enthusiasm.

Through upgrading my limiting beliefs, I altered the beliefs that no man would want to be with me in my *imperfect state* and that people would misunderstand me because of my expressions being strange. This was freeing.

Through the practice of re-programming limiting beliefs, letting go of the past, making time-sensitive goals, practicing a strong visualization practice, and with good nutrition, exercise, forgiveness, and very hard work, I felt a true rebirth and return to innocence. I started seeing my real beauty beyond the body. It truly radiated from the inside. I was gifted with new eyesight; physically blurry, but spiritually clear.

Now, eight years later, I continue to feel more sexy, wealthy, and in love from the inside out! I never got the eye surgery and my face is about 60% healed. My heart remains deeply grateful for the *sexy intuition* that has been guiding my way the whole time, both then and now.

I share this story today because you have the very same life-force potential living within you. *Know this, live this!* We all have our unexpected journeys. *They chose us and we chose what to do with them.*

So, whatever circumstance you are going through, don't let it define you. Your being is eternal, powerful, and capable. Follow your unique road to success by implementing what *feels right* to you. And if you don't know what feels right yet, keep listening in the silence and you will have instincts. Ask the Universe to help you discern and to give you the strength to *proceed and succeed*. And you can.

Many blessings to you!

About the Author

Renee Airya is one of the industry's most highly regarded healers. After an adventurous decade of three near-death experiences and then emerging more enlightened, Renee now dedicates her life to helping others awaken to their own *sexy intuition*, gifts, and power. She works with women to enable them to become more confident, comfortable, and sexy in their body, business, and relationships by dissolving roadblocks to success. She is on a mission to ignite the spiritual and financial security of 100,000+ women across the globe by 2014.

She is the founder of Sexy, Wealthy and In Love and the Big Bang Breakthrough Healing System.

http://www.reneeairya.com

HOW KUNDALINI TORE ME APART AND PUT ME BACK TOGETHER

JJ Semple

When I activated Kundalini in 1973, there was only one book on the subject: Gopi Krishna's masterwork, *Kundalini: The Evolutionary Energy in Man*, published with little fanfare in New Delhi in 1967. At the time, I had never heard of Kundalini.

In 1971 I had gone to France to study music. By 1972, however, I was tired of drugs, alcohol, and sex; all the worldly enticements Paris offers. For one thing, I wasn't making progress with my music, except to realize I wasn't very good at it. My teacher, Steve Lacy, a well-known jazz musician was the first to recognize it: "Your problem isn't musical; there's something wrong with your breathing. It's not related to music. The music just shows it up."

I had practiced yoga for six years, knew breathing exercises existed, but had never tried them. *Galignani's* on the rue de Rivoli had the most extensive supply of books on yoga and meditation, but none of them seemed to fit my situation. The day I went there, a young girl was browsing through the same bin I was plowing through. She asked me what I was looking for. How this young girl led me to *The Secret of the Golden Flower* and my eventual deliverance is well-documented in my book, *Deciphering the Golden Flower One Secret at a Time*. I won't rehash my tribulations, except to say this encounter and my subsequent practice of the meditation method in *The Secret of the Golden Flower* not only changed my life, it changed my Being.

How did it happen? The book this young lady gave me was a manual, not much different from the one that comes with a DVD player. Only this book was a set of instructions for a meditation method predicated on deep breathing. How I got from learning to breathe deeply to a change of Being required a lot of detective work and perseverance.

"What do I mean by Being?" you might ask. Being is not our limited perception of *the human being;* a statistical measure, a medical record. Being is the physical and metaphysical components that make up an individual; the energy that animates the body as well as the body itself; the ethereal and the material.

The first technique in the method – learning to breathe without hearing my breath – led to an encounter with something greater than my physical body. As I practiced the breathing, I felt my body swell beyond its confines, as if another body, albeit an invisible one, surrounded me. This was my true body – my Being – connected to an infinite, but invisible, world. For some reason my physical body didn't fit perfectly within this ethereal body, as I was quite certain it was meant to. I wondered if this was the cause of the breathing problems Steve Lacy had detected.

With practice, I began to take in more air with each breath and the number of breaths per minute decreased. More air with fewer breaths. Why is this important? A turtle breathes three times a minute. The average human adult: fifteen times. The turtle outlives us by hundreds of years. My heartbeat slowed to almost half its normal rate. What's more, as I progressed, I understood my breathing problems were due to a childhood injury that had not healed because I failed to report it. Not only was this meditation changing me physically, significant insights on my past, present, and future life came to me spontaneously.

Although my consciousness was in my physical body, it co-existed outside of it. I could move it around and steer it. If I chose to move it outside my body and never come back, that might be too bad for my body, but it wouldn't be the end of my consciousness; *that* was eternal. It resided inside me for the moment, but I knew it had existed before my current substantiation and it would continue to exist after.

One day, I felt a stirring in the lower belly, a build up of energy. A few days later, I detected the property of direction in this energy, down the back and up the front in a circular motion. I remembered the words: *backward-flowing method.* It was a phrase I'd skipped over many times in *The Secret of the Golden Flower* because I didn't know what it meant.

I interrupted my meditation to look for the passage. In two quick flips, I located the text: "At this time one works at the energy with the purpose of making it flow backward and rise, flow down to fall like the upward spinning of the sun-wheel… in this way one succeeds in bringing the true energy to its original place. This is the backward-flowing method."

For months I had been deciphering the book bit-by-bit. Each technique had to be mastered before moving to the next. An interlocking series of dependencies. Now I had reached the final step. Should I decide to reverse my breath, intuitively, in my mind's eye, I saw my physical body conforming to the infinite proportions of the Being that surrounded it. I saw my childhood injury corrected by the power I was unleashing. I was part of an energy field, limitless, formless, and all-encompassing.

Somehow, an atheist like me had crossed the line in the energy continuum, from physical to metaphysical, all the while trying to remain an objective observer as to the nature of my experience. My immersion in a greater consciousness was real, the byproduct of precise physical exercise whose purpose was opening up hidden resources in the body. I saw no hand of God; no religious overtones in anything that had happened. In fact, the experience wasn't really spiritual. No ritual, no prayer, no invocations, no learning of doctrine, and no chanting the names of saints.

Moreover, what happened to me could happen to anyone, should they follow the method. I saw no barriers; no cultural, no language, no geographical limitations. No religious prerequisites either. An individual could do this if they were a Christian, a Jew, a Muslim, a Buddhist, a Hindu, or none of those; one with no religious affiliation.

It took another month for the Kundalini to activate completely, for the breath to draw the energy in the lower belly up the spine into the brain. But I was no longer controlling the process. I was no longer doing it; *it* was doing me. And as soon as it reached the crown chakra, the Kundalini took over my body.

Using the nervous system, it inventoried every aspect and particle of my body. It discovered the malformation resulting from my childhood accident and began to correct it, directing life force energy to the afflicted areas. That was forty years ago.

I have lived with a permanently active Kundalini ever since. Hardly a day goes by when it doesn't open up some new vista: a physical issue needing attention, an insight into some weighty subject, an out-of-body excursion. It has literally torn me apart and put me back together the right way. Much of its work is physical; a great part is metaphysical, during moments when my consciousness leaves my physical body.

These are special moments, but do they have real world relevance? For despite the wonders Kundalini confers on an adept, as long as we inhabit bodies, we are prey to their demands. Can Kundalini help us manage these demands?

Yes, especially demands that are really addictions, physical ones like alcohol and drugs that harm the body. Kundalini does not tolerate self-abuse. Unlike a pre-Kundalini body, a Kundalini-active one is sensitive to ingested substances, including harmful foods. How do I know what to avoid? My body gives me immediate feedback. Early on I learned to trust Kundalini; it knows what's best and it has never led me astray.

Over time, Kundalini also helps control psychological addictions, like gambling, spending, shopping, eating, and sexual excess. It leads you to make the right choice.

Stuff happens as you move through this practice. Outsiders won't believe you, but that's because they don't practice. Don't look for validation in the outside world because you won't find it. It's been the same for material scientists. Some of the greatest have been called quacks. This didn't deter scientists like Nobel Prize winner, Dr. Barry Marshall, about whom one eminent colleague commented, "I thought the guy was a madman."

To prove his theory about ulcers, Marshall used his body as a laboratory, ingesting a bacterium that causes ulcers. He took the antidote he had devised, thus proving his theory and silencing former critics, who now praise him.

"We scientists should have looked beyond Barry's evangelical patina," one critic said, "and not dismissed him out of hand." The gentleman who called him a madman said, "Science needs solid research, but it also needs someone with great vision. Barry had vision."

What does this have to do with Kundalini? Every time someone begins a Kundalini practice, they use their body as a laboratory in the pursuit of a goal conventional wisdom considers imaginary. Why do they do it? They do it because they have glimpsed the continuum and they want to prove, if only to themselves, that it is real; that consciousness is tied to the simple, autonomic act of breathing.

So what is Kundalini?

Kundalini is evolutionary biology, an energy reserve within each body. When the body begins to wear down, it's there like a warranty that never expires.

In evolutionary biology, a phenotype is an organism's observable characteristics or traits, such as its morphology, biochemical or physiological properties. Kundalini is advanced evolutionary biology, in that it changes an individual's phenotype characteristics during a single lifetime. If Kundalini can modify phenotype, will the surge in Kundalini awakenings not create a gene pool variation capable of influencing natural selection?

Because we lack critical mass, we may not be able to verify the process today, but that doesn't mean it isn't happening. We are speeding up evolution because Kundalini affects brain chemistry, and brain chemistry affects phenotype. Kundalini is included in our bodies for a reason. If it didn't serve a purpose, evolution would have eliminated it. That's how evolution works.

Today, there are hundreds of books and thousands of articles and websites on Kundalini. There are hundreds of people practicing all sorts of Kundalini-related techniques today. What caused this surge? Doesn't this explosion of interest validate the topic?

Many see Kundalini experiences as unscientific and mere anecdotal accounts. Because I'm a scientist, I would love to agree with them (and I did before it happened to me). Now I can't, in spite of my inclination to do so. Why? Because my practice opened more than the doors of perception. It put me inside the energy continuum. I can only describe the results of my practice, how it changed my Being by:

- Triggering autonomic self-healing mechanisms capable of correcting defects due to neural degeneration.

- Rejuvenating brain and body as a result of intense neuroplastic activity.

- Retarding the aging process.

- Reversing self-destructive and addictive behavior.

- Heightening and enhancing consciousness by awakening various metanormal powers.

- Refining the Being to the point where the individual is able to affect a release from karmic bondage.

- Demonstrating clearly that the ego spirit persists after death.

- Helping to end dependency on ineffective health care models.

- Facilitating the transition into the next state of existence.

Having so many books on Kundalini nowadays is a blessing and a curse. Many are written by individuals who have never had a Kundalini experience. Lots of information is *not* the same as accurate, reliable information.

If you believe we have reached the pinnacle of human evolution, Kundalini is probably not for you. If, on the other hand, you are certain that we have only scratched the surface of human potential, there is a way to find out: start breathing as I did. You just might awaken Kundalini.

About the Author

JJ Semple is the founder of Life Force Books, a publishing company that features books on the neuroplasticity aspects of, and guidelines for living with, Kundalini. He is the author of two books on Kundalini and its effect on human evolution. His first book, *Deciphering the Golden Flower One Secret at a Time*, is a memoir of his Kundalini awakening. His second book, *The Backward-Flowing Method: The Secret of Life and Death*, takes an expanded look at a meditation method for activating Kundalini in a safe, permanent, and repeatable fashion.

JJ Semple's formal education includes studying English Literature at the University of Pennsylvania and George Washington University, and earning a master's degree in marketing from *Hauts Etudes de Commerce* in Paris. His personal study involves yogic and meditation practices inspired by *The Secret of the Golden Flower* and a variety of teachers and adepts, including Gopi Krishna, Milarepa, and Lao Tse.

http://www.lifeforcebooks.com

"I'M SORRY: THERE'S NOTHING WE CAN DO"

Misty VanderWeele

"Dear God, no! Not my little boy!" my mind screamed. *Why me! When is this pain going to stop?!* It seemed like ever since I graduated from high school, life had dealt me one hard knock after the other. From a new marriage that shouldn't have happened, a miscarriage that had me rushed to the hospital hemorrhaging, the death of my father who I never really got to know, and then a final blow, or so I thought: a divorce. How could life get *any* worse?

After tumbling around single for a few years, I got the answer.

With something unbearable, almost intangible in the sense that *things like this only happen to other people*, I sat there listening to the doctor tell me that my brown-eyed, little boy would die from the most common paralyzing, incurable muscular dystrophy called duchenne. Images of crippled children flashed before my eyes. *He would be lucky to graduate high school.* I was left with the feeling of *how could this be happening?*

The pain expanded through my entire being. It was deafening in my ears, forever leaving its mark on my heart.

After a week lying in fetal position begging and pleading with God I had a conversation that changed… everything. I had what I call my *ah-ha* moment. The small voice inside my head said this was happening so I could help other people; that through this painful journey of watching my son live in the face of this tragedy of duchenne, I was being called upon to give back. I didn't know what that was going to look like or even if I could deliver. All I knew was somehow I was to do this.

As I came to grips with what was happening, I set out to prove I could do something about it by giving my son the best quality of life that I could. I might not be able to take the duchenne away but I'd be damned if I'd let it take me or my son's happiness away too.

During this time I married an incredible guy, followed by the birth of our beautiful daughter. You could say I threw myself into living my life always looking for exactly how I was going to help others. I did some public speaking, dabbled in fundraising, and worked on self-improvement as I watched duchenne ravage my son's body over time. He stopped walking when he was eleven, had a full spinal fusion back surgery by fifteen, then had a heal cord lengthening and toe-tendon release surgery.

Before I knew it, my boy was a senior in high school getting ready to graduate. And he did. But it was not for long before he got severely sick and went to the hospital, fighting to not have a permanent tracheotomy (a tube placed through a hole in his neck down into his lungs so he could breathe).

I put aside how exactly I was to use this emotional rollercoaster journey with duchenne to help others. I knew it was time to write my son that book I'd always wanted to write for him. This is exactly what I did. I wanted to honor his life while he was still here gracing mine. I wanted to capture his life essence to be remembered for all time. Titled *In Your Face Duchenne Muscular Dystrophy All Pain... All GLORY!*

In Your Face also reveals eight very important life skills needed to not only live life successfully but to cope in the time of any tragedy.

Skill One: One Foot in Front of the Other

In other words, live one day at a time. Know that there are going to be bad days. Even the best of us feel sorry for ourselves from time to time. Only allow yourself to be in that spot for a short time. Know that life doesn't miss any one of us.

Skill Two: Heal Your Life

Do whatever you can to fix your *issues* whether it's codependence, living in a healthy body, or managing your anger. Ask for help if you need it. Get over your pride. If you aren't at your best and doing well, how the heck are you supposed to help others and live your life as happily as you can?

Skill Three: Get a Different Point of View

When life gets overwhelming, take a deep breath. One thing for sure is that there are numerous ways to look at things; there is always another opinion. Sometimes another perspective on life is all you need to make the right choice for yourself and your family.

Skill Four: Get Realistic.

Peel all the drama out of the situation at hand and get real. I refuse to live in that spot of *oh poor me! My son is going to die* mode. Realistically none of us knows when it is our time to go.

Skill Five: Live for Today with the Future in Mind

"Today is a gift, that is why today is called *the present.*"

Do the best you can with the blessing and knowledge you have right now. Be happy to be alive. Yes, taxes are due in April, so keep those books in order all year so it's less stressful and so that you can enjoy life even then.

Skill Six: Life Goes On; Change Happens

Change is inevitable so the quicker you can accept it, the faster you can get on with being happy. Life goes on no matter what.

Skill Seven: Always Look at the Bright Side

Purposely look for the beauty in life and expect to find it. I promise you will.

Skill Eight: You Can Do Something About It

Remember you have a choice even if it's just choosing to think positively. Or you can be more of a rebel like me and not take no for an answer.

Through writing and publishing three duchenne books, I realize my calling of helping others was waiting for me to gain the experience I needed in order for me to fulfill it. It's as if I am being Divinely guided.

Not only has my son graduated high school, he is twenty years old… and alive!

About the Author

Misty VanderWeele is a duchenne advocacy and support specialist, author of three duchenne muscular dystrophy books, *In Your Face Duchenne Muscular Dystrophy… All Pain… All GLORY!*, *Saving Our Sons One Story at a Time* and *Saving Our Sons & Daughters II*. She is dedicated to creating global recognition for duchenne: the most common, paralyzing form of muscular dystrophy. Duchenne affects about three hundred thousand children world-wide; every year up to six hundred are newly diagnosed. Two a day die from complications. Life expectancy is mid to late twenties. There is no known cure.

Misty teaches hope is a life skill of purposely looking, finding, and then holding onto the beauty of life.

http://www.mistyvanderweele.com

TRANSFORMATION FROM WITHIN

Nicole Rigato

Becoming a Healer

With a background in events management and marketing consulting, you can imagine that becoming an energy healer and spiritual teacher was the furthermost thing from my mind. I was however extremely dedicated to my path of self-discovery and personal development and, having felt the suffering of others ever since I was young, I felt a sense of urgency to find answers to alleviate their pain. I could also see patterns in my life of recurring events and situations that were creating suffering for me, and I knew there was a reason for this that I didn't yet understand.

I was barely eighteen when I took myself off to see a counselor and this was when my journey truly began. I spent many years soul-searching, researching, and studying different healing modalities, and I was blessed to be mentored by the most diverse and amazing teachers from all around the world.

The biggest key for transformation occurred to me when my life, my marriage, and my body fell apart all at once and I spiraled into deep despair, bedridden with illness and depression. I felt like I'd been punched in the chest when my doctor gave me an ultimatum telling me that if I didn't make some drastic changes in my life… I was going to die.

I was left with only two choices: move out of *victim consciousness* into empowerment and heal myself or leave the planet. Thank God I chose the first option! It was then that I made the commitment to myself to find, beyond the pain, the ego, and the stories that my mind had attached to my suffering, who I truly was.

When I was told I needed to have a fourth operation because my reproductive organs were covered in cysts and adhered to my uterus with adhesions and endometriosis, I asked the doctor to give me three months grace to try alternative options. I couldn't face more surgery and I realized that I couldn't keep having stuff *cut out* of me. I realized I needed to heal from the inside out and heal the cause, not the symptoms.

It was time to face my deepest fears that I had worked so hard on burying my whole life.

In the days, weeks, and months that followed, I learnt what true surrender meant. I realized that I was terrified of feeling the unresolved emotional energy that I had stored in the cells of my body because if I allowed myself to connect with this, I would not be able to bring myself back from rock bottom again.

I was still consulting part-time, I was caring for my partner at the time who had testicular cancer that had spread throughout his body, and I was studying a diploma of energetic and spiritual healing. I did a mental detox, I followed a strict diet to re-alkaline my body, I walked in nature most days, and I explored different energy healing modalities to support me in releasing all of the trauma and unresolved emotional energy that was making me ill. I felt a deep heart connection with one of my teachers and she held a safe space for me to start letting go. Some of it was deep emotional pain from my childhood, some of it was trauma from being raped when I was a teenager, and some of it was connected to memories held from past lives that were still creating fear in my being.

I needed to treat myself as a whole because even though the major cause of my illness was emotional, I had to work with all parts of my being because they are all interconnected. I had to learn how to nurture myself for the first time in my life and every day I dedicated time to focus on expanding and exploring my spiritual connection. When I returned to my surgeon four months later to have more scans, there was absolutely no trace of any adhesions, no endometriosis, no poly cystic ovaries, and all of my organs were back in a happy place within me! All of the theories I had learnt, all that I had read and talked about, now became my concrete reality because it was my own personal experience.

Healing From Within

For many years I looked outside of myself to feel whole, to heal, and to find the love that I was disconnected from within myself. When you *do* find this connection to your own Divine self, it is more fulfilling than anything you will ever find outside of you.

The grace that flows into your life when you live in connection to your heart is incredible. The deeper I went into my heart, the more answers I found, the healthier I became, and the more rapidly my healing abilities and spiritual gifts evolved. My financial situation also improved, I finally became aligned with my purpose, and I learnt to live in a space of connection with my heart as opposed to being controlled by my mind. My mind was very powerful so I had to be aware of bringing my attention to what I wanted to create in my life, rather than what I did *not* want.

The more developed your consciousness becomes, the quicker you manifest what you are focusing on. I'm sure you've heard the saying: "Be careful what you wish for." My mind became a tool that was guided by my heart. I practiced surrendering doubt, fear, and challenges that I perceived as unsolvable, even when my mind protested.

When we do surrender our fears and doubts, we tap into the infinite wisdom and the flow of Universal consciousness that holds every possibility and opportunity for us. We release the contraction from our mind and our being that keeps us feeling small and separate, and we become open to receive much higher solutions which are in resonance with our heart and the truth that it holds for us.

The Balance of Love and Power

In my experience, I have found that some souls come to this world grounded through their heart whilst others are grounded more in their power. Those that come in grounded through their heart have a journey to learn about their own power. While those that come in grounded in their power have a journey to learn about their heart.

The beautiful beings who are grounded through their heart unconsciously feel and process all of the unresolved energy for their family from a young age and they find it difficult to say *no*. They also give tirelessly but feel unworthy of receiving (unless they've earned it), they carry an enormous amount of responsibility, and they feel very disempowered in their relationships. They can often start to feel resentful because their needs are not being met. They burn out because they give with the best intentions but they give from a place of feeling depleted, not from a space of complete fulfillment allowing Divine energy to flow through them as the vessel.

Sound familiar?

When you open your heart and ground your personal power with love… whoa look out! You become an unstoppable force of creation!

Be Grateful for Life's Painful Experiences

Gratitude is such a powerful energy for healing.

One day, I was working with a lady who had been sexually abused as a child, lost her dear father suddenly, became physically ill, felt disconnected from love, and lost all of her self-confidence. As I worked with her, I related to all she was experiencing and held a space of deep compassion, non-judgment, and unconditional love for her. I held a space for all of the parts of her that didn't feel lovable or worthy of receiving love and created the safety for them to return to wholeness within her.

I held the absolute certainty in my consciousness that she would heal and become empowered again, because she was ready and I had done it. I knew how to support her to make the transition from where she was then to where she wanted to be.

During our session, I had a flashback of the challenges in my life and, in that moment, felt enormous gratitude for all of my experiences, mostly the painful ones. I felt gratitude for all of the opportunities I had to forgive and to all of those who hurt me deeply. I also felt gratitude to my teachers who reflected what I needed to heal within myself.

I have studied many different healing modalities and paths. But I truly believe it is my own personal experience of having to heal myself that allows me to support my clients from an authentic space.

And I am eternally grateful for this.

The Gift of Healing

Through this journey of healing from within, I have been privileged to witness everything from fractured faces heal in front of me (avoiding three surgeries) to *incurable* diseases cured. With all the work I have done to empower myself, I have watched my family transform. We also hold in our consciousness past fears, traumas, physical disease, and beliefs that have been held through many generations of our genetic mothers and fathers.

When our ancestors are unable to resolve such negativities, they continue passing them on to us through our DNA and we can unconsciously create our life and relationships through *their* filters still expressing through us. When we do resolve them, we access the gifts and talents that were also held through our lineage.

I worked with a beautiful little boy who was going blind because of a genetic condition held by his mother. It was a condition that the females in his family carried that send the males blind. I predominantly worked with him and did some work with his mother, as she was the carrier of the gene. His sight started returning and to do this day, his vision is fabulous. The ultimate test was when his mother and father gave birth to another boy and when they had the genetic testing done, there was no trace of this gene anymore.

When you heal, the benefits will flow on to your parents, your children, your siblings, and those that are connected to you through your genetic-energy body.

I have finally found who I am and I have learned to love and accept myself. This is an ongoing journey that I am excited to explore more deeply. I am no longer afraid of my feelings (I choose not to view them as either positive or negative) and embrace them regardless of how I feel. Emotion is just *energy in motion*. When we don't allow this emotion to be expressed, it becomes trapped in the cells of our body.

The changes in my life continue to be profound and I feel incredibly blessed to be entrusted with this divine mission. There is no quick fix if you want the changes in your life to be permanent. You must transform your energy and your consciousness; self-discovery and healing is a life-long journey. It will immeasurably enrich your life! If you feel that you want to create change in your life, explore the infinite depth of your heart to find your life purpose.

Know that you are fully empowered to do this.

Bring your attention to the Divine synchronicity occurring all around you, guiding you to these doorways of opportunity when you ask for guidance or assistance; no one else can tell you what your truth is.

May your journey back home within you be deeply blessed.

About the Author

Nicole Rigato is an energetic and spiritual healer, teacher, and author who focuses on empowering her clients in all areas of their lives. She does this using a combination of intuitive counseling and energy healing and is passionate about creating on-line programs, group healings, and guided retreats to support the expansion of one's energy and consciousness.

Nicole is also an official casa guide taking regular guided retreats to see John of God in Brazil.

She takes a loving and compassionate approach to encourage opening the heart to find one's own truth and aligning them to their life purpose. She also mentors people through awakening their healing abilities and unique soul gifts whilst supporting them to integrate this into their life and career path.

Nicole is currently based in Melbourne, offering private consultations in her healing clinics in both Sydney and Melbourne.

http://www.nicolerigato.com

HIDDEN TREASURES

Sahaja Coventry

The number for tomorrow's lottery is 741. The number for tomorrow's lottery is 741. The number for tomorrow's lottery is 741.

Her voice had a quality somewhere between an angel and an airport announcement telling me which gate and at what time to board.

Yes, I really did hear this voice in a dream and bought a lottery ticket the very next day. That same night, New Year's Eve 1980, my jaw dropped as those very numbers rolled on the 7 p.m. lottery draw. My mind stopped and time just didn't make sense.

A spark of amazement and awe at what is ultimately possible ignited.

At this time in my life, I knew nothing about the Law of Attraction or the power of manifestation. All I knew was that I had a great longing to go to India to meet a spiritual master. I didn't have the money, but prayer and passion I did. And in one dream, I was given the numbers that produced my $1,048 win, which was twenty-four dollars more than the airfare. This connection with a Source that could give me information from the future made my head swoon. What a miraculous gift and the money was the least of it.

In looking back, this was my first undeniable and indisputable meeting with grace, spirit, the Universe, and Source. That could and would have been a wonderful end to the story and the beginning of a miraculous life, but it wasn't. I still had some major life lessons to experience, particularly in the arena of physical health. I was going to need to draw on this experience and connection with Source many times as my life unfolded and took me on the healing journey I hadn't anticipated.

Dealing with illness is a very personal story. There isn't one way to heal or theory that fits all illnesses. It is rather more like a puzzle that each person must unravel with hidden clues and treasures very specific to them. I chose to follow the riddle, decipher the clues, and not pass the responsibility to heal over to the medical profession *or* the natural healing profession. I must add that I was happy to accept support from both when *and* where I was guided. I simply recognized my self, my body, and Source as the primary healer.

I have heard it said that the illness itself is the healing. Now that's a Zen koan if ever there was one. I understand now the truth in those words. Traveling through this journey has culminated in a sense of wholeness, integration, and many more moments of peace and connection. It is no coincidence that the word *heal* comes from the same Latin root as *to make whole.*

By sharing my story, I would like to show how that which completely took away my life as I knew it became, in truth, a redirection to all that essentially matters.

I woke up one morning in Bali, twelve years after that trip to India, with the room spinning. Never had I been chronically ill before, so I just assumed it would pass. Days turned into weeks and ultimately months… then years. Every medical examination showed nothing except a latent immune weakness after experiencing Dengue fever a year before. Diagnosis when there is no explanation: chronic fatigue syndrome.

The symptoms were unimaginable. In retrospect, I don't know how I managed to spend nearly two and a half years bed-bound. Had it only been fatigue, it would have been easier. Suffice it to say, there were ten-day monthly episodes with symptoms that resembled the original virus.

I remember one day walking (and I use that word loosely) through the Jarrah forest in West Australia where my partner used to take me to a weekend cabin and leave me for days. I so desperately craved solitude and silence. That day, I was struggling. In utter despair, I cried out to the same Source that miraculously gifted me once to now guide me to heal and to show me what I needed to see. Tears streamed down my face. I felt an embracing presence and from that day, humility and surrender became my ally.

The first thing that came to me clearly was the need to change my diet. I hadn't lived a very conscious life in regard to what I put in my body. I completely resonated with the teachings of macrobiotics that say illness is the byproduct of being out of balance with nature, and that returning to a natural lifestyle and diet begins the healing process. I wholeheartedly embraced cooking with love and reverence for the aliveness of whole grains, organic land and sea vegetables, beans, and more. Even though I had no energy to do anything, somehow I had the energy to teach myself every aspect of this wholesome way of cooking.

After the first two years and after following the advice of a trusted mentor, I began teaching macrobiotic cooking. That might have been the only thing I accomplished in a week, but I made sure I was prepared and present for class each Saturday morning. If I needed to rest for the next three days to recover, so be it. It had become a priority and a passion.

Amidst these years of healing I continued to have setbacks and episodes that took me to deep spaces within. Each challenge required that I dig deeper inside to feel whatever emotions were there. It required me to discover and challenge my limiting thoughts and beliefs and to find deeper reserves of faith and trust.

My macrobiotic teacher reminded me one day that there are no straight lines in nature. The healing process also doesn't happen in a straight line. I found this to be true and a deep teaching. I had many ups and downs; many zigzags. It is very human to feel hopeless when things appear to be moving anywhere but forward.

This led me to another beautiful teaching that health is not a goal, but a direction. If you are making the supportive, positive changes in diet, lifestyle, and thinking, then you are moving toward health. Not being fixated on the goal allows for a deeper relaxation and trust in the body's innate capacity to heal itself. This relaxation creates the optimum environment for healing.

We all know whether we are moving toward or away from health. If we are honest, the signs are always there. If we keep our intention on the desired direction, there is a deep peace and trust that can ride out the downward loops of the spiral. It also helps to have a friend, beloved person, or support network who can remind you again and again of the bigger upward spiral when needed.

Perhaps my biggest personal challenge in healing has been to embrace the truth that everything changes. When I hit a dark space, a part of my mind was absolutely certain it would remain forever. And when I moved into a positive space, I deeply wanted to cling to that and never let go.

Through the years, I kept observing that no matter what showed up, everything came and went. Every headache, every feeling of helplessness, every high energy day, every feeling of invincibility, all of it... passed. Not one thing, except for the space where all of this was happening, remained. I began to recognize this space as the open awareness where all emotions and experiences come and go. It was the space of infinite freedom.

Eight years into my healing journey, I still loved teaching and continued to observe my fluctuating energy levels. I began to study macrobiotic counseling. Within a few months of starting the course, I sincerely and consistently embraced the dietary side far more than when following my own spontaneous self-taught version. My previous eating with its zigzags was a good example of *no straight lines in nature*. I lost weight and gained some energy. So excited experiencing the results, I felt certain that I would soon be full of vitality.

And just the thought of how amazing that would be filled me with such joy and hope.

Once again, this could have been a happy ending or a lovely long plateau of well-being, but it wasn't. I soon discovered a lump, and the diagnosis came: I was facing a life-threatening disease. My mind did back-flips. I couldn't fathom this. I knew in my heart of hearts I was on track. It didn't compute. After the initial shock, I got a sense that perhaps with my increased energy level and health, I would be able to deal with the underlying condition that had probably been there for a long time.

No longer did I feel that healing only required eating more brown rice and leafy greens and all would be well. It was more like following a treasure hunt. What would be the next clue? Where would I be guided next? Again, I asked for help big time.

I accepted minimal surgery and continued on a healing diet. I was also led to a book that deeply touched and inspired me called *The Journey*. Here, I learned about cellular memory and about how early traumatic experiences and negative emotions that are shut down in the body can lead to illness or negative behaviors later in life. Children have a sensitivity; what isn't an issue for the adult can be perceived very differently through young eyes. I committed to this process where I would dive in many times to meet the unfinished emotions and issues from my past and to find resolution and forgiveness. With such an elegant and powerful guided introspection, I could see the results as health began to return.

I couldn't believe I hadn't been more aware of the impact of negative emotions on health. I had already done a lot of personal work and meditation in my life. This, however, took me to a very real place inside that I hadn't previously accessed.

I knew I had to train to become a Journey practitioner™. I felt I had found the two most important aspects to help myself and other people heal: like flying with two wings, addressing both diet *and* emotions are equally needed. The clarity and grace that resulted from my commitment has been a great gift.

In the last six years of facilitating many beautiful souls' journey processes, I have learned much more. As previously stated, we all have our own healing path. Each is unique. I no longer *sell* what works for me. I am more interested that each person connects with their deepest knowing; that infinite awareness that guides us on our individual paths.

I am currently embracing the truth that all bodies come and go, and that healing's highest purpose isn't just about sustaining physical life. It is about finding this connection with the loving Source that guides us. It is to help us realize we aren't separate. Life cares for us and leads us to our individual paths to awaken to who we really are.

No doubt life can be gritty. I bless my healing journey for all that it has and continues to awaken in me. I invite you to encounter your *self* with all that it reveals. There is nothing within to be afraid of. At the center of the darkness is a light that can illuminate any hidden fears. This light can guide you to what is needed moment by moment. It can shower you with trust and appreciation for all that you have. There are many hidden treasures if you are willing to explore.

From that first voice in my dream to the ongoing nudges saying wake up or *wrong direction* to the showering of daily blessings, there is only one constant: love. Love is what heals. Discovering this all-inclusive love that has never left, not for one moment, this is the ultimate treasure and this is what heals.

About the Author

Sahaja created her business, The Great Life, in 1995 where she is a macrobiotic educator and alchemical wholefoods cooking teacher. She studied macrobiotic counseling with David Briscoe, one of the finest counselors in the field today. She is also an accredited Journey practitioner™ and trained in visionary leadership and conscious coaching with Brandon Bays and her husband, Kevin Billett.

Her background includes a bachelor's degree of fine arts in graphic design and a master's degree of expressive art therapy.

All qualifications aside, Sahaja has been through her own healing journey which has imparted a sensitivity, compassion, and wisdom that she generously shares with her clients and students who are undergoing their own transformational journeys. Her love of truth is above all else, and she is available to support and assist each person to find their highest potential, their Divine spark and ultimately their Source of being which is unconditional love.

http://www.thegreatlife.com.au

ALL OF ME

Suzie Palmer

The journey of unfolding ourselves seems endless. The urge for an inner healing trek often begins before one is even born – mystical karmic records portend time and again. To set out unraveling, seemingly indelible scars that occur in our infancy, childhood, or teenage years, on top of possible past life issues, presents an almost impossible climb.

But, that's what it takes. One must climb the impossible climb to heal at the innermost level.

It's said that the emotional body is the most difficult to heal. A whole gamut of problems such as allergies, energy imbalances, and a myriad of dis-eases, can be resolved physically. Yet, we hold on to latent emotions and reasons for their development as if our entire essence depends on them. Call it *familiarity breeds content* or *better the devil you know*, but subconsciously, we have identified with unhelpful emotions for so long that living without them doesn't seem an option.

Until you reach rock bottom and arrive at the liberating state of *sick of being sick*.

The law of gravity shows that what goes up must come down and the teachings of Buddha dissuade us from the potential suffering caused by flying too high. It also appears that we need to arrive at our lowest ebb to attain true and lasting liberation. Healing revelations can be found in that dark, lonely place and it's our glorious freewill that got us there.

I'm sure not everyone plunges to their deepest depths of despair and helplessness before soaring along their paths. However, we all experience some version of it, and for me it came sixteen years into a physical challenge before becoming really fed up with losing the freedom mobility brings. I'd been working on maintaining equanimity of my mind for so long – thanks to Buddha's teachings once again – and holding onto my faith in a psychic forecast given by a mystical sage many years ago that I had neglected the need for constant action. In 1999 the sage foretold that a simple healing remedy would be found when I was *really ready*. Despite symptoms worsening over the years, I finally became ready in September 2010.

And there began my real exploration of healing from within…

Countless physical healings by means of alternative therapies had been ongoing over the years, as well as eating healthily (without many restrictions), spiritual healings that also delved into the physical, emotional, and mental levels, and meditating sporadically. However, I hadn't plunged into my healing 100%. I hadn't committed all of *me*, unconsciously downplaying the immensity of my quest. Finally awake and prepared for the challenge, I wasn't going to let any idleness be to my peril.

As shared in the *I Am That I Am* chapter in *Adventures in Manifesting – Health and Happiness,* I refused all advice given by neurologists when I was diagnosed with multiple sclerosis in 1995 at twenty-four years of age and continued to dismiss medical advice that told me to take drugs I didn't feel comfortable taking. From the moment of diagnosis, I had asked the professor for guidance on vitamins and alternative therapies, and sought advice on how to avoid another attack; but, anything outside the prescription arena wasn't in his domain so he dismissed my hopes with a wave of his hand: "Ah, they won't harm you, but they won't help you either."

The world I knew changed in that instant. Up until then, I'd imagined specialists were equipped to provide some assistance within their field of expertise. After undergoing extensive and expensive tests that led to an indefinite diagnosis, I assumed some help would be offered. Instead, I was suddenly digesting information that could be considered a death sentence. Such depressive reverberations didn't ricochet around my mind and body, I'm happy to say. Somehow, a deeper inner knowing that all would be well played in its place.

Mum and Dad were by my side that day, powerfully adding to my positive outlook. Mum was saying, "I know you're going to be okay. I just know it." And Dad said, "The ball's in your court and we're the ball men." He also said I was the best person in the family to get such a thing, because he strongly believed in my ability to cope. "And anyway," he added, "you wouldn't want your mother to have it, or me... or your brother and sisters would you?"

I wouldn't wish it on anyone.

Ironically, eighteen years later, I do wish my health on everyone! My inner health that is! In September 2010, when I finally took my health seriously, I embarked on a totally new lifestyle. Morning and evening, I commenced drinking green smoothies - a varying concoction of approximately 60% fruit to 40% leafy green vegetables blended in a high-powered blender for supreme digestibility. I ate a variety of fulfilling salads for lunch with nuts, hummus, seaweed, olives, and other raw tasty treats. My body began to crave my new daily nourishment and my health quickly bloomed in gratitude.

As within, so without. I intended to become so strong on the inside that my exterior self would inevitably follow suit. On investigating the eating habits of our closest primates and then adopting their diets into my life, I began to believe that I could potentially be as powerful as a human can be, even if only a smidgen on *make love, not war* bonobos, apes who are as close as 98.8% to our DNA – closest you can get to being human without being one. Horses and elephants too survive on only greens and fruits. The strongest earth animals with their gentle nature, demonstrated to me the very reason I needed to embrace healing from within with all my heart and soul. Inspiration to be as strong as I could be compelled me more than ever.

It all made sense. Our ancient bodies are encoded with an innate intelligence that has guided us to survive through thousands of years, the vast majority preceding cooked food. I needed to reactivate that knowledge, get back to basics, simplify my life to the core of my being so I could get out of the way and allow the body to heal. My new approach of eliminating all modern day eating seemed extreme to many of my family and friends, but as we know, extreme circumstances require extreme measures. The only exception is a weekly treat of baked potatoes and pumpkins.

Although our bodies are of the earth, our spirits are Divine and I knew my spirit was the driving force keeping me healthy and well, despite being unable to walk freely for fifteen years. It sounds paradoxical: healthy, spiritually wealthy, yet unable to walk. But that's how I've been along my healing trek, and my focus remains on walking again too.

I imagine I am walking and that very act engages the same motor and sensory programs that are involved in actually doing it. Everything our immaterial minds imagine leaves material traces, so that the more we imagine moving, the more tangible the benefits of imagining become.

In the book *The Brain That Changes Itself* by Norman Doidge, MD, an experiment was conducted showing how muscles can be strengthened simply by imagining using them. Two groups of people exercising a finger muscle were studied. Monday to Friday for four weeks, one group imagined they were doing trials of fifteen maximal contractions with a twenty second rest between each, while imagining a voice shouting, "Harder! Harder! Harder!" At the same time, the second group actually performed the exercise.

The results revealed that the subjects who had actually carried out the physical exercise increased their muscular strength by 30%, as expected. However, those that had only imagined doing the exercise increased their strength by 22%. The reason lies in the motor neurons of the brain that *program* movements. Doidge says that "During these imaginary contractions, the neurons responsible for stringing together sequences of instructions for movements are activated and strengthened, resulting in an increase in strength when the muscles are contracted."

You only have to visualize moving in your mind's eye for your brain to transmit precise orders to the rest of your musculature to prepare the movements and ensure the necessary co-ordination. Movements imagined and then felt, produce measurable physiological effects, causing the body to benefit from the exercises one is visualizing.

Only a few minutes' visualization a day enables immobile people to maintain physical energy. Imagining me as glorious, strong, mobile, and agile develops these qualities by creating mental, virtual images that are vital to their attainment. Thereby, laying the groundwork for the fruits of my imagining to blossom... This is so encouraging to me!

Together with visualizing, I do isometric exercises that involve muscular contractions without changing positions, which are perfect for me. My upper body is so strong; I am blessed to have the tools to keep it that way, as well as having the tools to strengthen any largely unused muscles through my current lack of walking. Daily, I celebrate my actual ability to transfer, stand for periods (albeit supported), and take some steps with my walker.

In order to regain strength and agility throughout my entire body, I perform mental gymnastics as often as possible. My only battle in this arena is maintaining a steady routine, which makes the exercise even more authentic remembering my past inner struggles in maintaining enthusiasm to work out. I walk, run, climb, skip, dance, somersault, tiptoe, swim, and do yoga in my imagination during meditation in the morning and sporadically throughout the day, all the while chanting affirmations such as, "I am healed. I am walking. I am vitality. I am health. I am a miracle. I am Source. I am abundance of every level," and wonderfully on.

Following are the last two verses in a poem called *My middle name is Mary* I wrote to give to friends at my recent 41st birthday party. It commences with an Audrey Hepburn quote: "Nothing is impossible, the word itself says, 'I'm possible!'"

> *They say when you know your limits and*
> *try to stay within them you are free*
>
> *For me, my physical limitations collide with*
> *my mind's limitlessness, so I live quite contrary*
>
> *Well, my middle name is Mary and we all know the nursery rhyme*
> *So in response to, "How does your garden grow?"*
> *I enthusiastically answer, "Fine!"*
>
> *I'm re-sowing all my brains maps with neurobiology*
> *It's a neuroplastic phenomenon, with mental gymnastics I'll find liberty*
> *Seems an ongoing process, the end goal firmly in mind*
> *So, please send your healing vibrations, perhaps*
> *then I'll be walking in no time...*

As you can see, my explorations and determination to bring about complete physical healing is resolute, and I dismiss any shadows of a doubt whenever necessary. The emotional aspect to possible causes to my challenge is so slippery to grip. However; the best investigation I've come across so far is *forensic healing*.

This technique discovers the how's, why's, where's, and when's underlying the development of my physical challenge. It detects negative life and emotional patterns, as well as belief systems that developed when I was very young and became a tangible aspect of my adult life. And also, it determines profile ages when life-changing thoughts and beliefs rise.

Through switching on the light and revisiting events when one is younger, amazing freedom from unconscious oppression is uncovered. Again, wonderful affirmations were given to me. And I feel lighter every time.

Soon, I'll be flying instead of walking... so, I've slowed down on *forensic healing*, and surrendered to the belief that I chose to experience this at some point in my life before I even came here, long before any unsettling emotions in childhood.

So keeping my heart on my healing goal, I absorb Michelangelo's advice: "The greater danger for most of us is not that our aim is too high and we miss it, but that it is too low and we reach it."

About the Author

Australian author and poet Suzie Palmer is considered by many to be a true inspiration. Her work can be found in numerous international publications. Suzie's first published poetry, *Loving All*, was followed by *Prosperity Rat*, an illustrated book of haiku. Her writings have also appeared in the *Adventures in Manifesting* series. *Come Fly With Me*, a collection of Suzie's children stories, led to invitations to give presentations at schools and motivational talks at workplaces. Suzie also performs her poetry at events, usually accompanied by live musicians.

She is currently writing her autobiography while working for world-peace, love, and humanity.

http://www.suziepalmer.com

HEALING THE MIND, BODY, AND SOUL

Gaye O'Brien

For many years I had been living in denial, believing that if I just kept pushing ahead things would turn out alright. Well, surprise, surprise, this wasn't the case despite working harder than ever, but perhaps not smarter. I was putting all that I had into my career, family, and home life.

Upon awaking one morning, I had the sudden realization that things in my life were not okay. I had a visit to the doctor that revealed the tell-tale signs of burnout; high blood pressure and insomnia. At that moment I realized I had not been listening to my body for quite some time. It simply had been full-steam ahead in the survival mode of life.

Just at that moment there was a glimpse of information on a television advertisement about a health retreat. I immediately contacted the company for more information. Sometime later, when the brochure from the retreat arrived in the mail, it included some interesting facts about meditation and its benefits. The benefits of improving sleep patterns and developing better concentration levels caught my attention immediately.

I began meditating in earnest. It became part of my daily routine which I still continue today. The increased awareness resulting from this discipline of meditation allowed me to witness my mind, body, and emotions. It also allowed the spirit to begin working through me.

The continuous practice of meditation has given me the ability to develop an incredible focus on what I want, which includes being passionate about the people in my life. I started working more meaningfully with my body. I rekindled my interest in yoga, which only compounded the benefits of my meditation practice. Through this combination, my body is now so much more alive with energy.

This added agility obtained through my yoga practice has helped me overcome a major physical challenge.

Healing With Visualization

Several months ago, I was attempting to get out of my car and my knee was so badly swollen that I could barely walk. An MRI revealed that I had a torn cartilage, tendon, and ligament. Bed rest, reading, writing a book, nutritional supplements, massage, Bowen therapy, acupuncture, and meditation became my necessary treatments, per my beliefs in healing.

Over time, I learned to use visualization along with regular glucose injections to increase the strength in my joints with the building of new connective tissue, and mini *trampolining* to energize the lymph system.

Visualization is a great practice because it utilizes the power of quantum physics. It causes the mind to view items and situations as if it is really happening; it can't tell the difference between fact and fiction. This is what makes it such a powerful tool in healing from within your spirit to manifestation in your life.

According to quantum physics, the body is not solid and is made up of millions of tiny vibrating particles. There is much space in the body to enable cells, which are currently maladjusted to move into alignment, with positive thought vibrations.

Conventional medical wisdom said I needed to have surgery, which would not really solve the problem itself, but only temporarily remove the symptoms. The surgery intervention would also cause nerve damage, according to some patients' research. I was also informed that it may take up to two years to fully recover. The medical specialist that I went to see however told me that it would only take a minimum of four days to recuperate. This was very conflicting information.

I actually got quite excited when my knee initially swelled up, because I knew that pain in the body could be a direct result of stored negative emotions waiting to be released, according to the ancient Hawaiian Huna healing tradition. Here was the perfect opportunity to perform healing on myself through the energy channels in my body. I knew I could repair my knee by envisioning the healing light of love moving freely through my spiritual body.

Healing and the Mastery of Mind

Healing from within requires the mastering of the mind, which is made up of two very important parts: the *thinking mind* (10%) and the *doing mind* that includes emotions (90%).

Our conscious, or thinking mind, processes information in an interesting manner. As the information enters the mind, humans can only process a tiny piece of all the sensory input available, which is why we are all so individualistic. If the synthesis of the information is wise, it will be filed in an efficient manner for convenient use at a later time by the unconscious mind.

Being conscious is about creating a destiny – being in charge and not simply allowing events to unfold randomly.

I have planned goals in all areas of my life, including health, wealth, career opportunities, business and family relationships, and spirituality. The life that is being experienced today for everybody is a direct result of the seeds that were sown some time ago in our minds.

Be proactive. Take the initiative and watch, hear, and feel the magic begin in your life!

I had the chance to reflect on my life through the healing process of my knee. I was able to spend time reading, researching, resting, sleeping, and visiting with family and friends. In fact, I was able to do all those things that I didn't think I had time for in my life.

Many people would see a torn cartilage as a real issue or problem. I saw it as an opportunity to further heal my life!

Even after the healing of my knee, I continued the detoxification of my body with renewed vigor and healing energy. I later learned from naturopathic tests that my body was acidic and more green foods were the answer to heal my liver. I have taken this advice in combination with my healing practices.

Why had I been manifesting disease in my body?

Because my unconscious mind was saying, "Listen to me." By being presented with health issues, I was fortunately forced to work with my body. Many people don't think like this. They may have been brainwashed to block out the pain, or believe that it is bad, or something that has to be cut out of the body. I found homeopathic pain relief very effective, as well as an NLP technique called the pain paradigm. This process allows concentration on the areas where there isn't pain in the body so it can have the effect of defocusing local soreness.

The Power of the Unconscious Mind

The unconscious mind runs the body and initiates all the actions that we perform. We don't have to think about it. Isn't that amazing? Once we know how to do something, it happens automatically, whether we like it or not. The unconscious mind will deduce from the experiences and act upon them in a very efficient way. Information that has been incorrectly interpreted or labeled in a person may have to be reprogrammed in order for that person to have a more fulfilling life.

I have spent much time exploring ways of uncovering, loving, and shredding through the data unwisely stored in my mind. The practice of daily meditation is a gentle way of doing this because the *baggage* is simply released over time.

Self-hypnosis is another useful method to release this burden from the unconscious mind. Once the spring cleaning has been done in the mind, the correct information can be reinstalled with a healthier view of life.

NLP presuppositions provide some very useful beliefs with which to work on as well. This includes such ideas as *you are doing the best with the resources you have available to you at the time*. This is a very empowering concept indeed! It moves away from the *blame game* allowing healing to occur. The problem is diagnosed and it is possible to move forward into a healthier sphere of life with the finding of a solution.

Having spent many years learning to manage my emotions has helped my internal healing process significantly. Emotions are an incredible device that is very useful. With observation, I have noticed that my emotions go up and down according to the sensory stimulus to which I am exposed. I can go from anxiety about the future or a family member to despair or worry about a particular problem in a split second. Many different emotions can be felt over the course of a day.

My practice has been to allow these emotions to just be and not react unless placed in an extreme situation where it may serve a very useful purpose. For example, adrenalin associated with fear comes in very handy when it gives extreme strength and energy to escape a dangerous situation. Quite often though, emotions simply have the habit of consuming vast amounts of energy for no good reason. I have found that the use of techniques such as taking a step back, exercise, seeing something from a different angle, focusing on love, and showing gratitude can be a great means to manage emotions effectively.

Mastering Emotion and Reframing Self-Talk

Reflecting on our thoughts and emotions is happening at all times. What we reflect outward returns to us. That is why when we are feeling happy and full of love, the whole world seems to be on our side. Emotions offer a wonderful opportunity to learn something interesting about ourselves. It can help us redefine our higher purpose in life. Emotions are to be kept at a constant state. We must learn to master them before they master us!

This is why self-talk is so interesting. A lot of the auto-suggestions that surround my healing could have been, *"Why did it have to happen to me?"* or *"What did I do to deserve this?"* In my particular situation, I decided that what I needed was lots of physical therapy, rest, time to contemplate, peace, quietness, and self-kindness. I tapped into the knowledge of many amazing therapists who assisted me on the road to recovery. One of the major things that I learned during this period was to ask questions and seek help. Often times people are very keen to help, particularly in their area of interest or expertise.

Negative things that are said to oneself are a direct reflection of the unwise processing of information from current situations or the past. The stories that one tells oneself have to be rewritten if one is to experience a healthy future of great manifestations. With awareness, love, and a focus on the present, this scripts life. It allows life to be rewritten and the unconscious mind to be transformed.

Reframe the negative self-talk. Practice positive affirmations daily to keep positive energy of love flowing throughout your inner body; your spirit. All new habits can be consciously learned, practiced, and used regularly before it becomes automatic in the unconscious mind. Surrounding oneself with people who are conscious, or willing to become mindful of their experiences, is very useful in reinforcing new and empowering habits.

The fun really begins when we finally realize that we are not in control of our lives as we would like to think we are. By learning to go with the flow of life's circumstances, we adopt the flexibility to allow the life force within us to work through us and not against us.

Know Thyself

Be adaptable, like a tree blowing in the breeze, while still following your chosen path. I knew that spirit was in charge of me during my knee recovery, and this awareness has helped me through the times of pain, loneliness, and discouragement. It has graciously taught me much about myself and my life purpose.

I have certainly learned to know my mind, body, and soul more intimately than I would have done without having gone through this experience. I have a renewed vigor and hope for my life. The more we are able to release the baggage from the past, forgive, listen to our bodies, love, and trust our inner wisdom of intuition, the more we will grow spiritually.

The gift of the future awaits you!

About the Author

Gaye O'Brien has a bachelor's degree in education from Central Queensland University of Australia, and has taught in the education and training sectors.

She conducts leadership workshops for teachers and businesses, and is the author of *NLP for Teachers: The Art of Encouraging Excellence in Your Students* and is also a Co-contributor to *Entrepreneur Success Stories: How Common People Achieve Uncommon Results Volume II.*

Gaye is also a business and success coach, NLP practitioner and trainer, Passion Test facilitator, and trained Demartini Method facilitator.

She lives with her husband in Yeppoon, Australia, and has three children who have all grown into beautiful adults.

http://www.gayeobrien.com

THE POWER OF RADICAL SELF-CARE

Lee Chamberland

When I was sixteen, I almost died laughing. I was very drunk and sure that if I had taken a good run at it, I could have jumped over a very large bonfire. Well, I made it half-way, and fell right into the center. I remember trying to lift myself out of it and finding it very funny that I couldn't. The next thing I knew someone was yanking me hard, pulling me out, rolling me around on the ground, and managing to put out the fire burning in my hair and clothes. Soon after, I was on a hospital bed being treated for a third degree burn. The next day I was told that the fellow who pulled me out of that fire was the only person within shouting distance at that moment. If it wasn't for him, I'm pretty sure I would have died laughing.

I share that story to give you a small picture of my less-than-stellar beginnings when it comes to living with abundant health and happiness! Before the bonfire event, I had experienced a serious episode of depression at fourteen and quit school at fifteen. By the time I was twenty-one, I was tired and scared. I'd been smoking, drinking, and partying on a daily basis for many years and had experienced a *lot* of drama and drinking related madness. In fact, I knew it was a miracle I'd made it to twenty-one alive!

It was at that time that I met a woman named Sharon who would change the direction of my life in a big way. She was my boss and I admired her deeply. One day she spoke seven words that transformed my life. "Lee, you are so bright. You are amazing!" I could tell that she believed it. Talk about the right words at the right time! To Sharon, it was just a passing comment.

To me, it was a reason to live.

Within two months I earned my GED credential (high school equivalency) and started my first year at college, absolutely terrified that I didn`t have what it took to succeed. After all, I had quit school at fifteen and barely passed tenth grade! On top of that, the words of one of my junior high school teachers haunted me. "Lee, if you quit now, you`ll never amount to anything."

Thankfully he was wrong.

In those early college years I raced everywhere I went; every moment felt like a giant race to some unknown finish line. I was terrified that if I slowed down, I'd fail. I was desperate to achieve and find a place to belong. I also lacked the knowledge and skills needed to set healthy boundaries and take care of myself. As a result, my health took a serious nose dive. My immune system became so weak, my body so inflamed, that a series of doctors told me they didn`t know how to help me. Finally I found a doctor of naturopathic medicine who said, "Are you under much stress?" Incredibly, I was so out of touch with myself and my health that I told him I didn`t think so!

That was another critical turning point. It was one that helped me discover my true passion and calling. The more I discovered about the power of equipping myself and others with outstanding health and happiness tools, knowledge, and support, the more excited I got. That was also the beginning of a radically new life for me; one with abundant energy and authentic happiness. Today, I stand amazed that I am not only still standing, but thriving.

Now, after twenty-five years of expanding my own health and happiness and helping others to do the same, it's very clear to me that if information was all that was needed to be healthy, happy, and *whole*, more of us would be living fabulous lives with optimum well-being. We've watched enough TV shows. We've read many excellent books and attended a lot of workshops. Instead I believe we're often overloaded with information and lacking the right tools and support to apply it in our day-to-day lives, and maintain it over time. The truth is: With the right tools and support, we could drop our addictions to TV, to overeating, shopping, gambling, and to staying too busy to notice how deeply sad and tired we really are.

And yet, we`re all doing the best we can with the knowledge, tools, and support we have right now. We`re all just walking around trying to get our needs met. That's what we do. If we don`t have the tools and resources to meet our needs in healthy ways, we attempt to meet them in unhealthy ones. For example, if we`re overcommitted and tired because we haven`t learned how to kindly and clearly say *no*, we might eat or drink something sugary to get a boost of energy. If we`re stressed out by all the worry we feel and we haven`t learned how to question our stressful thoughts, or how to use relaxation techniques, we might go shopping and spend money we don`t have. . If we want intimacy with another human being and haven't learned intimacy skills, we often end up doing or saying things we regret.

Thankfully, however, everything I learned in the school of life, in the classrooms of excellent universities, and via working with so many wonderful clients over the years all add up beautifully. And so, when I reflect on what it takes to manifest higher levels of health and happiness, one vital thing stands out: it's clear to me that if there were only one thing each of us could do to live a great life, it would be to practice radical self-care. Why? Because, we're all designed to naturally live great lives… *when* we're truly well.

The best of everything good flows more freely from that place of well-being. It also flows more freely out to the world because whatever we do for ourselves, we also do for the world. In fact, we are everything we bring to the world. We can`t possibly bring any more than we are!

So, when I say *radical* self-care, I mean beyond the norm. Far beyond that. I mean revolutionary. I mean, imagine what most folks in North America do for self-care… and then do more. Because, as you may have noticed, a great many people today are experiencing a serious shortage of energy and an unfortunate abundance of chronic illness and worry! And because, as Einstein said, if nothing changes, nothing changes.

Radical self-care gives us the vitality and energy we want to do the things we want. It rejuvenates us deeply. It naturally connects us to our passions and purpose, to our inner wisdom, and to feelings of calmness, relaxation, and ease. No matter where you are on the wellness continuum right now, with just one more self-care action, your ability to heal, thrive, and serve others is enormously enhanced.

The excellent news is that there are many outstanding self-care tools available to us today. The ones most of us think of include physical fitness, eating whole foods, getting good rest and sleep, and drinking ample water. Yet there are a host of additional self-care tools that will help you heal and create increasingly fast shifts to higher levels of health and well-being. These advanced health and happiness tools act powerfully to turn stress into relaxation, dysfunctional relationships into healthy relationships, fear into love.

They are the tools that I use to enhance my own life and those I invite, and help, clients to add to their toolbox when the fit is clear. A few of the best ones include the ability to forgive (yourself and others), question stressful beliefs or stories, weave fun and play into your life, live a life connected to your passions and purpose, and connect to spirit daily via meditation and/or prayer.

One of the tools I learned much later in life is how to live with my feelings and not run like the wind! Most of us were taught to run from what we perceive as negative feelings (sadness, anger, etc) and yet you may have noticed that what you resist persists. It takes a lot of energy, for example, to keep sadness or tears shoved down inside. The truth is: Crying is a beautiful thing because it is a reflection of what it means to be human; to have a heart. It cleanses what needs to be cleansed and connects us to our peaceful place. If you can't stop crying, then you could probably use the help a good counselor can provide. For most of us, however, we could instead use some practice letting tears or anger out in healthy ways. Most of us know that it's good to let feelings out, but knowing how to do that in a healthy way is another matter.

Here's one option: Take a few moments to tune inward, put your attention onto your heart and notice what you are feeling. Can you let the feeling be, give it some space, notice it without judgment. Practice this and you will notice that feelings come and go like ocean waves. Practice letting the waves come and go and notice that you feel better letting them come and go. And a bonus is that the energy it took to hold back the tears can now be put elsewhere, or simply enjoyed.

Practicing mindful breathing is also one of the most valuable things we can do to feel calmer, more focused, and more alive. This means taking a little time to quiet our minds' chatter, sit quietly, and pay attention to our breathing without judgment. Easier said than done for most of us. Yet, like everything else, we can get good at this with practice, and the benefits become noticeable very quickly!

Even three minutes of mindful breathing in the morning sets the tone for a calmer and more productive day. Set a kitchen timer (this may help you focus on your breath without thinking about the time). And when you notice that your thoughts are wondering elsewhere, practice gently returning your attention to your breath. In fact, learning to focus your attention on your breathing will help you get better at being able to concentrate on anything. Without focus, you can be easily distracted in the world we live in. With it, it gets easier to manifest whatever you want.

There are a lot of great tools for radical self-care available today, and in many ways it doesn't matter which ones we use, because a positive change in any area ignites a positive change in all areas. It matters more that we learn how to use them, and *then* use them. In truth, the journey of manifesting higher levels of health and happiness begins with one step. Take that step and you will notice that your life becomes lighter and more joyful all the time.

Finally, because I love to add a good *PS* at the end of anything I write, I'll add the following three important points.

1. Believe in your ability to transform in any way that is important to you. We`re here to love, grow, and evolve.

2. Ask for help. One day it occurred to me that *if you`re alive, you need help!* If you want to live your best life, you really need it. We all need it. There are no rules about who to ask for help or what to ask for, just trust your instinct and do it. Go for it. You will be glad you did.

3. Know that when you initiate positive transformation, the Universe will move mountains to help you. Watch and see.

About the Author

Lee Chamberland is well known for her remarkable gift as a speaker, teacher, and coach. She is authentic and dynamic. Her presentations are highly inspirational, fun, and full of powerful tools for manifesting higher levels of health, happiness, and well-being.

As a coach, Lee provides life-changing support to her clients. She helps them shift from just getting by to coping well, making wise decisions, and feeling empowered, healthy, and whole.

Lee is like a breath of fresh air – the moment you walk into her presence, you cannot help but feel good – her energy is cleansing, relaxing, yet invigorating. Working with Lee yields enormous positive results.

The Founder of Power of Wellness and a self-proclaimed *grateful student of life*, Lee has over twenty-five years experience and a lifetime of realizing that each new moment holds an opportunity for new beginnings.

http://www.leechamberland.com

TRANSFORMING MY LIFE ONE CELL AT A TIME

Laura Mayer

I was diagnosed with a disease that was supposed to get worse as I got older. But against all odds, I got better.

Shortly before my fiftieth birthday I looked out my glass door and said, "If I fell down I would never get up again. This must be what bone cancer feels like." I knew deep within something had to shift. I was losing my will to live. I was tired and, at that time, didn't know options existed. All I knew was the deep physical and emotional pain I felt as I continued to witness my body deteriorate.

I am a woman who, through trust in inner sources of love and acceptance, has transcended a crippling and supposedly fatal disease to achieve complete health and wholeness. Throughout most of my life, I suffered from anterior horn cell disease; a progressive, degenerative neurological condition originating in the gray matter of the spinal cord, which doctors told me would leave me completely crippled by age twenty-five and end my life by forty. Physically, this meant I was locked inside a body slowly collapsing inward, losing muscle mass in my arms and pulling the tendons of my hands into the shape of claws. I will never forget when the chief of neurology at a prominent New York hospital stood at the end of my bed and said in no uncertain terms, "There is nothing we can do for you, and the disease will continue to spread throughout your spinal column."

I was fifteen years old when I was given this death sentence.

My inner story was all about suffering. It took forty years of battling the effects of a crippling disease before I decided not to suffer anymore. After eighteen surgeries I made a decision to step out of the medical box and explore the world of energetic healing modalities. I was guided through that experience by remarkable healers, where I understood that the possibility of healing lies in the psyche and takes root where disunion between mind and body ceases to exist. Many others who face physical challenges stemming from emotional injury, as I did, might recognize themselves in my story.

"Either I heal or I'm out of here," I stated emphatically to the Universe, after a three-hour healing session with a medical intuitive/shaman from Colorado. She travelled energetically through my body, knowing me as if I handed her an MRI and my autobiography. She helped me to understand the deep-rooted emotional and spiritual pain running havoc in my cells, as well as empower me to have the courage to love myself enough and become the co-creator of my destiny.

Very soon I realized that healing was not just a physical event but rather deep, cellular in nature, and that the wounds of my heart would eventually heal every piece of my being and reveal my true nature.

I completely immersed myself in the world of metaphysics and spirituality. I made a total commitment to becoming healed; knowing with certainty there would be no short cuts and no magical cures. My belief was pure and my vision was guided. Nothing would stop me on my path. I studied various energetic modalities, attended spiritual workshops, and retreats. I read everything I could get my hands on that had to do with manifesting my life and healing my *self*. I spent time every day lying on my bed, holding a crystal, visualizing my already healed body. I brought the sensations to a visceral level knowing the Universe would manifest my vision.

I chanted daily to quiet my mind and to calm my soul. I visualized my fingers opening to the Universe as my body swayed to my harmony of my voice. I manifested perfectly healthy hands, felt the hot energy flow through them, and, as I sent loving healing energy to my hands, witnessed a shift as my body gradually responded and the tendons in my hands began to open.

Through activations and clearings on a soul level, I worked on shifting my body matrix to redefine *me*.

The Universe continued to guide me, sending me a plethora of gifted healers and angels. One of my initial healing experiences was with Jon, who emphasized the role of intention in healing, as well as the need to believe in oneself. As I lay on my bedroom floor I felt the energy flow through me from head to toe. Over the next four months I received healing from a man who sat three hundred miles away. Like others before him, Jon said, "You will heal completely, and you will bring healing to others." He told me that my spine looked like a train wreck.

I had suffered an injury to my brain when I was around five years old, which was likely the cause of the ongoing problems with my hands. My first healing session with him ultimately led me to believe that the dis-ease located in my spinal cord wasn't what the doctors had said it was. Rather, it had to do with deep-seated issues of abandonment and fear.

The healing messages were clear: *as I healed my soul, I would heal the phenomenon with me that had caused my hands to shut down.*

I told Jon I wanted to bring my story, my wisdom, and my open heart to children who were in discomfort or crisis. I was beginning to formulate a plan that involved working with families to open parent-child communication and foster understanding. I knew the etiological source of my dis-ease was deeply rooted in the belief that I wasn't loved.

"I have only one question for you," Jon replied. "Why aren't you out there doing it? The truth is that you wear your heart on your sleeve, which is an asset for the work you'll be doing. You have emotional issues to clear first, and then the physical will heal."

My next healing experience was with Carol, a seer from northern Virginia. Carol told me I should get ready for my life to change. "Everything you do in this lifetime will be aligned with the deepest compassion, which you'll express in the world," she told me.

But despite the steady flow of confirmations and affirmations from healers and psychics, I continued to deal with deep-seated issues of abandonment and fear that continued to present themselves. I yearned for my sister and mother's love, but I slowly recognized that opening to inner sources of love and acceptance was more important than receiving others' approval. As I stayed in my truth – my authentic self – I learned to allow others to be who they were and not how they responded to me.

As I became more in touch with the deep childhood wounding, doing what I call an excavation of the soul, I was able to release energetically those belief patterns embedded so deeply in my cellular make-up.

Soon afterward, I noticed I could move my left thumb. I was overwhelmed with joy, and a smile lit up my face as I said, "Thank you, God."

A wave of excitement ran through me every time I noticed that my physical functioning had improved in the slightest way. These minor miracles were but a confirmation that I was on the right path.

I drove to Boston to visit my hand surgeon, Mark, whom I hadn't visited in quite some time. I had postponed my annual visits because my hands were changing, and I wanted him to see me when my fingers were absolutely straight. I knew this would be a monumental moment for me.

As I sat in the examining room waiting for Mark, I felt excited and even a bit anxious. When he came in, we chatted for a few minutes, and then I held out my hands and proudly said, "Look at this!"

He examined my hands and said, "It's a miracle! Keep doing whatever you've been doing. This is truly a miracle."

Mark commented that my joints looked better, and he didn't see any reason why my hands wouldn't continue to improve. He was awestruck by how straight my fingers were. When he tested me with the dynamometer, used to measure muscle strength, my right hand went from zero to six pounds, and my left hand from six to eight. Encouraged by my progress, he believed I would continue to restore muscle strength.

"I always believed that the mind, body, and emotions were connected," he said. "And by the look of things, you've emptied out lots of emotional baggage you were carrying. I've never witnessed such a dramatic turnaround, and I simply can't explain it. I'm so happy for you!"

I hugged Mark and promised to return in a few years. As I closed the door behind me, a flood of emotions surfaced. This hospital where I had experienced so much pain and so much fear was now behind me forever.

As decades of physical and psychological suffering flashed before my eyes, I said goodbye to the Laura who was filled with disease and who needed medical intervention to survive. Energetically I felt different; I no longer belonged there, for I had transformed into a completely different person. As I drove away, I cried for the miracle that had taken place in my life. Having Mark witness my transformation was indeed a special moment for me.

As I continued to show up and be present, allowing myself to trust in something bigger than myself, I found that my own intuitive abilities exploded. I became deeply involved in energetic healing work. This was a gift given to me because I manifested complete healing. On this journey to the heart of the soul, I was finding my *true* self. These incredible experiences were awakening and enlivening my inner core. What started as a quest to heal my hands became an opportunity to awaken my heart.

I had healed enough to step out and become the healer I truly was.

When you lay down your weapons and pick up your angel wings you allow a softening to happen. You no longer *fight for your life*. You begin to see through different eyes and behold the world in a new light.

Healing from within was a process of releasing old messages stored in my DNA and learning what it meant to have the courage to love my *self* enough. When I started to trust that I deserved a better life and a healthier existence, my entire body started to shift into wellness. Mostly, I learned to *let go* and follow my inner guidance. In doing so I allowed my heart to be guided by intuition and grace; not by my mind or ego, which were, for the most part, driven by fear. I was slowly and steadily unlocking myself from the only existence I had known and began to vision a new life, filled with joy and acceptance."

I refer to this process as the K.O.R. Program because it must come from the *core of you*.

1. *Knowing* on the deepest level you deserve a life filled with joy, ease, and grace.

2. *Opening* to the unknown - stepping away from the rigidity of the past and welcoming in non-traditional methods of healing. It entails trusting that grace will step in and guide you and in the invisible lines of connection - even when you are clueless as to what will happen next. It is the ultimate trust!

3. *Releasing* or relinquishing old childhood patterns of belief that no longer serve you.

I knew that something had to shift and it did. I said *yes* and manifested a different life for myself. It is my prayer that my story of *healing from within* will inspire you to trust that you too can become the co-creator of your destiny, and live the life you truly desire.

About the Author

Laura Mayer, founder of SoulDancing Healing Practice, bridges her clinical expertise with her spiritual knowing. She is a spiritual transformational counselor, licensed occupational therapist, motivational speaker, and intuitive healer. She is a facilitator of Soul Memory Discovery and Spiritual Indigo Healing.

Laura's gift and greatest joy is in opening people's hearts and empowering others to be fully seen, fully heard, and fully present. Her work spans three decades as a licensed occupational therapist in the field of psychiatry and pediatrics. As a master healer, Laura's capacity to go deep within the soul will assist you in igniting your light to be the best you can be, while tapping into the source of pain dormant in your core. Laura is the mother of two indigo adult children.

http://www.dancingheartdancinghands.com

THE JOURNEY FUELS THE FIRE

David Saywell

More than once in this life I've found myself in situations I should be proud of. I should be overjoyed with the success I have experienced and content with all that I have. Yet, many times it's simply not the case. On many levels I know I should be. I know that for a friend, family member, colleague, or acquaintance, from the outside I seem as if I'm content and overjoyed. I also know that they have no idea.

Or do they?

Is there something you have always wanted to do that, for one reason or another, you have either never started or have left languishing half-finished? Are there times when you find yourself repeatedly doing something you really don't want to do, to the point where it affects you physically, mentally, or emotionally, possibly all at once?

If the answers to the above are a screaming *yes*, know that you're not alone. I've been there and perhaps there are also others out there who are just the same.

What I do know is that it's a part of life. This contrast, no matter how painful, is what we need to move beyond our current situations. We need it so that we could reach, leap, evolve, and blossom into our authentic, vibrant, audacious, amazing selves that we were always destined to become: to live the full expression of our soul's desire in the here and now. This is the act of living. We're here to grow. The most important, valued, and treasured gift you could ever give to yourself or anyone else is the seed of self-love.

The most significant turning point in my life unfolded only a few years ago when I was at a high point in my career. I was a senior project manager responsible of a team to deliver a large infrastructure project. It was my second role following a significant career change in industry and responsibility. For the most part it was challenging. Enough to keep me interested, I was on a steep learning curve and I was thriving. I even had aspirations of leading the entire team.

My family life was amazing. I lived in a wonderful home filled with a beautiful wife and daughter, and we were even expecting a new addition to the family. Even though I was working hard for long hours, we were having fun! Having kids is one of the best things we have ever done; they're a source of pure joy, amazement, and love. We have never laughed as much or as hard until we experienced life with our children. We can, and do, learn a lot from them.

Then it happened, gradually at first.

Although I didn't show it, I'd had enough. The interesting challenges had waned. The day to day had become mundane. I began to realize that the newness and excitement had once again (yes this wasn't the first time!) distracted me from what I really wanted to do. In the spirit of honesty, what I really wanted to do was but a mystery at the time. I had a general idea of what I wanted, but exactly what, I didn't have a clue! I felt like I'd allowed myself to drift along for the year and a half leading to this point. Even though I didn't know what it was, the path I'd taken wasn't aligned with my purpose in life.

With that realization, gradually my self-esteem spiraled and my negative self-talk set in. Physically, I began to suffer; tightness in my chest, shortness of breath, loss of appetite and Monday-itis (that started on Sunday morning!). I was irritable, moody, lethargic, and lazy. I'd been here before. I didn't like it and failed knowing what to do. And to add insult to injury, I internalized the whole ordeal. As far as those around me were concerned I had a great job, earned a lot of money, and seemed happy.

I started to question what my real purpose was. What was I passionate about? What should I do? It was demoralizing and didn't do much help, and in hindsight made things worse, to ask these questions and not get any closer to the answers.

Deep down, the turmoil, emotional unrest, and longing was moving me toward finding a purpose that was spiritually satisfying. It allowed me to care for and enjoy my family on a whole new level and get onto a new path as quickly as possible.

Intuitively, I knew I needed to talk to someone. As difficult as it was, I followed through with someone I trusted. The benefits and accompanying effects derived from this one small action were tremendous. I took a few hours off work just to talk. This was empowering because I did something for me and I was in control. I gained perspective by getting out of my own head and articulating my thoughts and feelings to another person. It started an ongoing dialog and I had someone checking in with me every now and then. The blockage of not being able to talk about my feelings was removed and I found it easier to talk to other people about it. This in turn created a web of support and a sense of freedom and control.

Having enough self-respect to take the time out, gain perspective, and give myself permission to do what I needed to do to be happy was the catalyst for change. I had sown my seed of self-love!

I'd been walking a lot in my lunch breaks but I was usually stressed when I left the office, and, if I was lucky, my mood was only slightly elevated when I returned. I felt better for the exercise and fresh air but it wasn't helping a great deal. For some reason I remembered the feeling I get when I'm just starting out on a holiday or road trip: a few miles in with the music cranking, windows down, wind blowing, and being absolutely on top of the world, singing as if nobody else can hear. I remembered how I would always feel thrilled, letting out a bellowing *yeeeeee-hah* or *wooooooo-hoo*!

So, here's what I did, just for fun: Every time I left the office, as soon I got to the stair well, I would picture myself a few miles into a road trip, with every fiber of my *being* being there in my car, exhilarated to be free!

Some people call it an ecstatic state; others: day dreaming. I called it a quantum road trip. My quantum road trips soon turned into quantum vacations. My one-hour lunch break turned to a four-week quantum vacation either to a luxurious resort or to a beautiful and serene location, always pushing the limits of my imagination.

I hope you believe this form of visualizing works. But if you're not sure, give it a go now. Just for a minute or two. My energy levels have increased tenfold just writing about it. Yours shall too! In moments like these during the day, I felt good.

Actually I felt better than good. I felt... great!

I'd decided to focus on what I wanted. I still had to work and if I was to, I was going to be satisfied. I knew that in order to experience a high level of satisfaction, no matter what, I must take pride in my work. If you take pride in your work, you will always do a good job and will always be proud of what you've done. Trust me. If you're proud of what you've done you'll invariably be satisfied. Universally, satisfaction of a well-done-job will always cultivate a vibrant self-esteem.

Now that I had liberated myself to a certain extent, I started focusing on my health. Instead of waking up and immediately dragging myself to work, I took the time to eat breakfast, even if it meant I would be a little late. I also stopped skipping lunch; after all, working hard and taking pride in one's work deserves a reward. So what I'd do was find a nice quiet cafe with good food and treat myself occasionally.

I was taking care of myself. I was so focused on feeling good and feeling happy that these feelings began to become a part of my day-to-day reality.

In the meantime my wife had been lovingly nurturing our second baby. The convergence of his birth and these new discoveries was life changing for all of us. Very fortunately, I was able to take some time off work to welcome our new son to the family and enjoy being at home. In between being a dad and husband, there was a small amount of time to reflect and really enjoy a new perspective on life. I'm still not sure whether it was delirium due to lack of sleep, intoxicated bliss at bringing a new person into the world, a moment of pristine clarity verging on an epiphany, or a combination of all those.

But what happened next defied all reasonable logic that we'd lived by up until this point. It was life-changing and one of the most amazing experiences we've created.

During the final days of my time off work, with the prospect of returning to a situation I wasn't enjoying, the desire to make a change and do something new became increasingly strong. The difference this time was that I felt good within myself. While pondering these feelings, I remembered a dream to travel that had been suppressed for a number of years. In fact, we'd talked about it several times, yet always found an excuse not to follow through. In hind sight, our past excuses couldn't possibly compete with a mortgage, toddler and a new born baby!

A group of our friends had been planning a six-week camping trip to Darwin and back for quite some time but up until now we had no plans of joining them. I mentioned the idea to my wife in passing and, by no coincidence, the very next day we decided to join our friends and travel to Darwin. But we had no plans for returning home; just an open ended six to twelve month window to do whatever we wanted. Within four days we'd re-shuffled our finances, ordered a camper trailer and four-wheel-drive vehicle, and hoped like crazy that we'd done the right thing.

I was quite emotional when I recalled the events of that week to my good friend and mentor. The ease with which it all had happened from deciding, getting a great deal on the camper trailer, finding the last vehicle available in our area to meet our requirements, to realizing and creating the resources we needed to make it all happen was staggering. The feeling of going from the extreme of being so trapped to total freedom was overwhelming to describe.

Needless to say, we followed through with six memorable months on the road travelling through some of the most remote parts of Australia's outback. It was an intense and spiritual odyssey allowing me even more time to reflect and gain a perspective I had never experienced before. I found the understanding and inspiration needed to motivate me in completing my first book, setting the stage for the next chapter of my life.

The journey really does fuel the fire.

"Find the road you know is yours. This life is love, and you the sun adores."

Sow the seed; nurture it and your life shall flourish.

About the Author

David Saywell is an author, poet and speaker with a self-described *unique take on life*. He writes and speaks on topics related to personal and spiritual development.

David has a heartfelt desire to share his experiences and work at the leading edge of creation in the New Earth, inspiring others to do the same.

Following an intense and spiritual six-month odyssey through some of the most remote parts of Australia, David now resides in a small country town, north of Melbourne.

Live the full expression of your soul's desire ... now! There are no limits. This is just the beginning.

http://www.davidsaywell.com

ANGELS IN OUR LIVES

Jacky Newcomb

"Mummy," my daughter called me, "look. A fairy-man!

My toddler daughter was pointing to a blank section of ceiling. How-ever hard I looked, I could see nothing at all. I lay down on the floor next to her and asked her what it was that she could see. Already, Charlotte was bored. The vision had vanished for her and she wanted to do something else.

Was she playing a game with me? Or was this a reference to the fact that her great grandmother had died two days earlier? Had great-granny come to say goodbye?

Is this a special story? Well, yes, it is special to me, but it's not a story in isolation. If the Internet is any indication in the current interest in angels and angel visitations, then the phenomenon is greater now than at any other time in history. Shops are full of angel pictures, stat-ues, stationery, books, and anything else you could care to mention. You can even *wear* angels in jewellery and clothing, especially t-shirts, which are worn by every second teenage girl and their mother (me included!) and are in every fashion store.

So what is causing this current interest? People seem to be having more mystical experiences in their lives right at this moment in history. Actually, if you explore the trend in more detail, you'll have to ques-tion whether people are actually having more angelic intervention in their lives, or if it is just easier for them to share these experiences now.

Most people have heard, for example of the near-death experience these days (floating out of your body at the point of death, seeing dead relatives coming to meet you, and meeting a bright shining light). Not only do people believe these experience, they almost *expect* them! You are unlikely to be ridiculed if you share your experience of meeting a guardian angel at the pearly gates, whereas if you go back in time even five years, it would have been harder to share your personal angel story.

Current day angelic encounters seem to fall mainly into two main types of categories:

1. **Comfort and Joy:** People in distress get a message telling them that everything is going to be OK. This type of intervention can occur whilst the person is in deep distress, when they are in a hopeless situation (a loved one is very ill for example), or a relative has passed away and the visit is from a spirit version of the person they loved, letting them know that they are OK but are in a different place. My own father came to me after he passed on. I spoke to him and asked him, "How are you, Dad?"

   His reply was humorous. "Well, I'm dead... but other than that I am fine!"

2. **Warning or Rescue:** A message is received sometimes as a human figure, or a calming sensation, just in time to save a life or prevent things from becoming worse! Or even more dramatic, people have felt themselves lifted up by unseen hands and literally pulled out of danger! I have received and read about many stories of children being safely removed out of the way of moving cars, or others who, following a horrific accident, awoke to find themselves in a new place of safety with no logical explanation as to how they got there.

   Not all stories are so dramatic and messages are often received as a strong intuition or nagging by a voice that sounded like mine. Sometimes the message comes as a series of colored lights or angel-type music – like this story of my own.

Music From the Healing Angels

When my daughter was eight years old, she picked up a tummy bug of some sort. It was late in the night and I had sat with her for many hours whilst she suffered. She was running a temperature and was exhausted. We both were! I decided that the easiest thing to do would be to make her a bed on the bathroom floor. She would be closer to the toilet and perhaps I could get some rest.

Anyone who has been without sleep for any length of time will understand this feeling. I was so tired I wanted to cry, and now I felt helpless too. What was I to do? I had read that if you ask for help, then an angel would give it to you. What had I got to lose?

"Please," I asked out loud, "if Georgina's guardian angels are out there now, can you look after her for a short while so that I can get some sleep?" What the heck, it couldn't hurt. I reasoned that I would be better able to cope the following morning if I had had some sleep, but really I was just tired.

It was then that I heard the music. I guess you could describe it as angel music – almost orchestral. I suppose if I was to say that it sounded like violins and harps, it would be hard to believe, but that is what I heard.

I knew that it was coming from within the bathroom, but I still could not believe what I could hear. I stood up to open the window (our house backed onto open fields and both of our neighbors were away) and I could not hear music outside anyway. I stood outside the door and the music faded away. It made significant impact on me that I decided to write it down in a notebook before getting back into bed. My daughter was indeed much better in the morning with no sign of a temperature.

This story sounded silly when I wrote it down. I almost decided not to use it. If I hadn't written it down at the time that it had happened, I probably wouldn't have remembered it they way it had unfolded. The brain has a funny way of turning something mystical or magical into something rational, even when it isn't!

How many of us have unusual things happen to them throughout our lives, which we are amazed at when they happen, but then we file away in the back of our logical mind?

I had a funny dream once where I had a very real visitation of a dead school friend. I was thrilled to see him and asked him why he has chosen to visit me. I guess I expected to be asked to pass on some important family information, but this was not to be the case.

His answer was something like, "I've come to see you because I can!" Not the earth-shattering answer that I expected. We embraced on meeting and parting and had a normal chat in between that I did not even record the discussion. Yet strangely, around fifteen years later, I spontaneously recalled our dream-like chat. My late friend was asking me if I wanted to write books about the experience I'd just had;

books of real life-stories of spontaneous afterlife communication. Obviously, although I had no recollection of the chat at the time, I must have accepted! Real life encounters of the other side have kept my interest for years and years and I have written a whole bookshelf amount on the subject!

Later, after sharing this visit with others, I discovered many who'd had similar very real dreams and similar visitations from the other side. One lady had a visitation from the deceased sister of her mother-in-law. The mother-in-law was (and is) quite ill and the deceased sister had popped in for a visit to express her concern at her sister's ill health. The purpose of these experiences seems to be to comfort the living, and it certainly does that!

So, what do you do if you don't have these experiences in your life but would like to?

How to Bring Angels into Your Life

Gradually over the years, I have discovered that there are similarities between the angel stories that have been shared with me. Many angel experiences have happened when people have been in extreme personal distress, but that alone is *not* enough. It seems that the experiences are most likely to occur when the help is asked for, or when people have literally *handed over* the problem to the Divine. It is almost as if the common element has been when people have said, "OK angels, I have had enough now. I will leave it in your hands."

Whilst I am not suggesting for one minute that angels are here as our personal slaves, it seems that they are unable to assist us without any permission on our part. So the trick is to actually ask for help, preferably out loud, and to be specific.

Why is it then that angels are not rushing around saving every life of anyone who is ill or involved in an accident? I wish I knew the answer, but at least it seems that sometimes we are able to ask for help and it can be received. Unlike TV magic, the results are not always immediate and the help does not always appear in the format which we may have imagined. Be prepared for something better or more suitable to occur in answer to your problem!

The help has to be in accordance with our current life path. Answers to *what are today's winning lottery numbers?* don't seem to be relevant or worthy of angelic intervention! Angels cannot always take away our pain. We are on a journey of learning and to step in at the wrong moment may prevent us from learning important life lessons.

Meditating

By meditating I have drawn myself closer to the angels over the years. I have found that for me, it is only by quietening my mind that I have been able to hear my inner voice, my guide, or angel. It does not matter which method you use, if any. I just sit quietly, usually with relaxing music playing in the background, and clear my mind.

Journaling

Incidences of angel magic started to increase once I wrote down any unusual dreams or strange coincidences in a journal (a notebook I keep by my bed). It wasn't until later, when I was reading through my experiences, that I found that the strange dream I had six months earlier was a warning or guidance for part of my life that is happening now.

Why not give it a go and bring a little angel magic into your own life?

About the Author

Jacky Newcomb is the UK's leading angel-and-afterlife-experiences expert, known to her fans the world over as The Angel Lady. She appears regularly in the national papers and TV as a paranormal experiences expert.

She's a multi-award winning, Sunday Times bestselling author with over a half a million copies of her books sold in UK translation alone. Jacky has thirteen published books (with two more out in 2012), plus meditation and workshop CDs, a DVD, and several packs of angel cards. Jacky is also a columnist, presenter, interviewer, public speaker, and workshop tutor.

http://jackynewcomb.webeden.co.uk

TRUSTING THE TIDE, LIVING IN THE UNKNOWN

Fiona G. Lyndley

"Matter must become Spiritualized; spirit must become Materialized."
Omraam Mikail Aivanhov

As a child, I had a clear knowing. I wanted to leave the world a better place than how I found it. I didn't have a clear structure or vision of how this would manifest. I just stayed open and now do all sorts of wonderful things; more than I could have dreamed of as a child!

I wonder how different the world would be if we asked ourselves two questions as part of our daily lives before every action we take. What would love say? What would love do?

How would it be if we practiced this as children, so that by the time we are adults we are able to invite a joyful and respectful conscious relationship inside of ourselves and with one another?

Could we all be recognized instantly as individuated aspects of the divine spark of life, whatever we have each learned to call the Divine?

I have always had the feeling that I am guided and loved by helpers in other realms. However, I have always kept this somewhat unmentionable to my family as it was evidence of my *wrongness* in their minds. I grew up in a traditional Roman Catholic family where from the start I experienced confusion. I was a child with fully active senses including extra sensory perception and could literally see incongruence as it occurred, whether in speech or action. I could see two streams of words around the dinner table, one coming out of people's mouths and the other from their belly area. It was also clear that the mouth words would not happen if the ones from the belly were heard, but I got to understand that I was the only one who seemed to hear or see them. I felt different from the outset and learnt that words are often superfluous.

My intuition told me I was being shown how to listen.

I started playing the flute at age eight, and learned that my perceptions of life held inside of me came out through music. My senses were welcomed in this medium by those who heard me. The paradox was that the more expressive my playing the more people received a connection to the love I felt.

Changes, seemingly uninvited, started to happen. I married my college sweetheart, earned my own living as a teacher, and appeared to be doing well externally. Internally, however I felt as if I were playing a game in a life that didn't fit.

I had three car accidents in three years; all involved people seemingly carelessly bumping into me, and each time the injuries became more intense. I now recognize this as a supportive life-force nudging me to dive into the panic within, because inside it was the life I had to reclaim. My marriage broke down as I followed studies in biopsychosociology and I eventually retrained as a registered craniosacral therapist, following trainings in Source process breathwork, soul response therapy, and body psychotherapy.

My heart and belief systems snapped apart. These belief systems included *marriage is for life* and *if required, you give up your own life to allow the life of another*. These beliefs had truly failed me and now I had no map or compass. No one in my family had been through divorce. Slowly, I began to reclaim my authentic life-energy as a creative loving force for changing myself and my world.

This was my first experience of living in the mystery of *the unknown*. I was not born into a family where living from this perspective was an option – or considered wise – but I felt myself waking as if from a long sleep.

This raised the next dilemma: Natural medicine was mistrusted or disrespected by my immediate family, so this period of my life served to intensify the wound of separation for being different. Whilst this was painful and lonely, it also served me to own more openly my deep sense of connection and love to the natural world. I learned to keep my own counsel to minimize the ridicule and criticism coming my way. I knew I was changed forever and I couldn't go backwards. My ability to stay present to what is and see beyond words was becoming a gift, as carrying this mindset allowed me to be as adaptable as I needed to be. Change, as I was experiencing, *is* the only certainty in life.

I went into deep internal questioning, examining my *wrongness* in the world, and because seeking help was seen as failure, the next fourteen years were some of the most painful of my life as they further separated me from my family. I was told I should turn to God instead! My own knowing however is that divine love is who human beings are and that God is Universal benevolence. This amused me: *I was* turning to God!

It was over a decade later that I manifested a wise teacher who looked at me one day and said, "But Fiona, you are a reluctant incarnate." *Finally!* This *was* an explanation for the constant desire to go home, the feelings of bewilderment as to how cruelly human beings can treat each other, the seventeen-year battle to not commit suicide, and the lack of my ambition. Finally the spirit energy in my body saw, understood, and gave me the fuel needed to continue.

I then had a spontaneous near-death experience in my mid 30's.

So how is it to die? It was painless. I had no sensation as I left my body; talking to the paramedics was the same as if you and I were standing next to each other having a conversation. There was a moment of feeling odd as I watched them working on my physical body and being unable to hear me while I was trying to tell them, "I'm here, I'm fine!"

I learned two things:

1. I hadn't completed what I was here for and, as I was shown, it was not my true time to transpire. I returned back to the earth quietly and peacefully in the ambulance.

2. Somehow going through that process facilitated me, relinquishing all fear. I also lost my defences. I came back having been technically dead for ten minutes.

I wrote a letter from this new place within me that I knew would change the entire family soul. It was written after deep meditation in this inner vulnerable soft place and, those that read it, who had also been hurt, wept as this was the energy they recognized in the letter. To those whom it was addressed acted in further denial and shutdown.

Love asked me to stay with those who had wept. I knew again at that point I had done my best. I had also addressed my worst fear and survived. My speaking up facilitated a death of an unhealthy connection and a birth of a loving connection and welcome within my place in the family, whatever my profession. My worst fear had been that if I spoke up I would be abandoned. I was; but only by those with whom loving communication was not possible.

From this new place inside, I made a decision to always find a way to honour my heart. My guides taught me in this place about compassion and healthy loving boundaries. I connected and arrived in a family where love is freely given and received. My reluctant incarnate syndrome has become a whisper of its former self. I have arrived here in Heaven on earth and now live life in a way that is connected in awareness to all life forms.

Here are some of the ways love whispered its messages to me:

When I travelled through Australia in 1998, I walked on a beach in Darwin and noticed tiny balls of sand flying and forming a beautiful shape that was a meter wide in each direction on the surface. I stayed a while to witness that it was a tiny sand spider creating this form. The lesson here: No matter how small you may be feeling in your life, you can still create spirit in matter several times bigger than your physical self.

Another time, I was walking another stretch of beach and cliffs, and the sea started coming in to a level that meant I was unable to retrace my steps. I breathed and just started walking and clambering over rocks. The words that came through me as I was doing this, I remember to this very day: "When there is no sign of a path, you must and can make your own."

That walk felt utterly prophetic at the time.

Another love message came from a retreat with Thich Nhat Hanh when I was given my Dharma name, which is Healing Ocean of the Heart. My time with him and the monks helped me integrate my inner and outer image of a family; eating, working, and exercising together in mindfulness. I shed many tears of reunion-grief mixed with such joy and gratitude of being given deep listening, teaching, and that of a joyous community. I really learnt that I can trust my heart, its longings and yearnings; it is *always* on my side.

I have many photographic memories of my travels. Another is of a long stretch of dry, arid road. The lesson I saw here is that the destination will arrive upon you if all you do is keep putting one step at a time along the road. Be present to the breath of every creation, whether human, vegetable, mineral, or the cosmos.

Have you ever noticed when sitting directly under a setting sun, everyone feels the rays are shining upon them? That is because it *really* is! So go sit facing west under the setting sun and you shall learn that you *matter*. Consciously choosing to visit places, people, and exposing yourself to inspirational events, will remind you inside that you too are a being who inspires... who breathes in and out. It is said that we all have a unique note, so go find your sound and note and let them out. Let yourself be heard.

Remember the little lights are as important as the big ones, so no matter what size you feel your light is, shine it. No one else can shine it for you, it is yours to shine, it matters, and it will be missed if you don't.

Take responsibility; be able to be responsive to be your most beautiful Innocence: inner essence. Life will soon show you if you are acting from a loving place or not.

So where am I now? Love has asked me to leave the UK, my birth land, and find my place to make my physical home. So with my beloved I am preparing to leave in the not too distant future.

In the meantime, I am teaching how to live in and from *the unknown* as a safe kind landscape, where spirit and matter commune in great intimacy.

I continue to see clients and I make it my personal practice to connect daily with my friends, within and without, so that I can take my part in co-creating a compassionate, peaceful world and fulfil my path that the young me wanted. I want to leave the world a better place than I found it.

About the Author

Fiona G. Lyndley is a successful published author of various articles and now this chapter. She has other books in the pipeline. She currently lives in the UK in joyous relationship with her husband and cavalier spaniel called Jasmine, where she runs a vibrant practice supporting the lives of those who find her.

She volunteers as a children's counselor at Childline and since August 2011 has been deepening into a *yes* commitment to finding her true physical home. To this end, she is travelling with her husband to British Columbia, the USA, Australia, and the Mediterranean parts of Europe, and hopes to be settled by the end of 2012. She loves cooking macrobiotic food for friends and family, practicing many kinds of meditation, dancing Nia and 5 rhythms, as well as going on vigorous cycle rides followed by lunch in a pub.

http://www.healingfromwithin.org.uk

RE-SPARK YOUR MAGNIFICENT SELF

Petra Hooijenga

*"All works are being done by the energy and power of nature,
but due to delusion of ego people assume themselves to be the doer."*
~Bhagavad Gita~

Do you remember the time when you were a child, looking at things with wonder and curiosity? Do you remember laughing so loud, you nearly wet your pants? Remember that time when you felt completely connected, and at one, with the magnificence inside you?

During those times, you were acutely aware of the love streaming through your heart and body, radiating and beaming. You could see everything and had complete awareness of every cell and atom in your body. In moments like these, you experience an amazing connectedness with life and with everything else in the Universe.

You were complete.

Within a split second, you could flip the size of your consciousness from a needle point to the complete Universe with all the galaxies, stars, planets, and interstellar space resting in their perfect and moving alignment. And you could flip it back again to needle-point size. You experienced the vastness of space, and peace in both the Universe and the needle point, and marveled at the greatness of this being and being at one with it. It feels like home.

As a ten year-old child, I used to go to this place. I would go there... almost every night. I would lie in bed, very still, and then concentrate very hard on a single point in my mind with my eyes closed. It usually took a few minutes of concentration, and then *pop*! It was as if I'd stepped through a portal into this Universe (my own magnificent one inside me) where I was at home and completely connected and filled with love, light, and power. I don't know how long I could've stayed in that state. I would flip back and forth between the Universe and the needle point; perhaps ten to twenty times, after which I would slide back into my normal consciousness into my bedroom with the yellow sunflower wallpaper and sunflower curtains, and I would go to sleep, happy.

I can't actively remember the first time I did it. I just remember being consciously aware of it at that age. I never spoke about it with anyone, as I assumed that everyone did it. If it was such an amazing place to be in, and it made sense to me back then, *why wouldn't anyone want to go there?!* Hence, my youth was filled with optimism, confidence, energy, and dreams about the future. Dreams about discovering the amazing world out there.

One evening, while I was still ten, I embraced my parents to kiss them goodnight and take myself up to the bathroom to get ready for bed. When giving my dad a goodnight kiss, I gently touched his forehead, and immediately retracted my hand because of the pain I was feeling.

"You've got a really bad headache. Why are you sitting here and not going to bed to rest?" I asked.

"How do you know I've got a headache?" he responded.

"Well," I said, "if I put my hand on it, I can feel the pain, and I can also feel it in my own head. Isn't that normal?"

By the reaction of my dad, I could tell that it was *not* a normal experience everyone else shared.

That evening, I went to bed late. My parents were intrigued, and keen to find out more about my ability to sense pain. If I could feel the pain, could I then also possibly take it away? If truth be told, I really had no idea what I was doing. It was the first time I had become consciously aware of it, and of course I was willing to give it a try. So, I thought, let's give it a go and just suck that headache and pain out of Dad's head…

And I did just that.

The only downside was that I now had the headache myself, and I had no idea how to get it out of me!

In the days, weeks, and months that followed, I noticed something had changed. I became conscious of being *different* from the people around me. Yet, by the interest and intrigue my little healing session had evoked, I also concluded that I was different in a good way. I concluded I had some special powers, and that this made me a very special person. So, on I went on my journey full of confidence and high self-esteem (and yes there was definitely an element of considering myself better than others). I believed I was great, and could do anything I set my mind to.

In my first year at high school, I put in a lot of effort, scoring straight A's in every subject. I considered that if doing well in high school was by my choice and effort, then I should always be able to tap into this ability if needed. So, for the rest of high school, I just did the absolute minimum requirement to pass, except for the subjects I was passionate about.

When it was time to consider university, I had my eyes on linguistics and journalism. However, it was the 80s and we were asked to deeply consider our future, making a choice that would allow us to make money, preferably lots of it. So, off to business college I went instead.

I was particularly attracted to situations where only the crème-de-la-crème would be selected, as this perfectly supported my beliefs. I moved from being chosen for my selective university, to being chosen as a national representative, and then international representative for AIESEC, the student organization I was an active member of. After this, between thousands of candidates from all over Europe, I was chosen as one of two graduate management trainees by a multinational corporation. I'm sure you can appreciate I felt really special, and I never hesitated blowing my own trumpet, sharing my *magnificent self* with everyone else.

When, at the ripe age of twenty-three, I was sitting at my big desk, as the interim managing director, heading up the Finland operations of this multinational company, it occurred to me: I have the power and choice to be who I want to be in this life. By making the choice and doing the work, anything is possible!

Reflecting back on the past five years, I realized I had achieved literally *anything* I had set my mind to. The sheer thought of it scared me shitless! But... who am I? What is this life all about? *I'm a managing director, but I'm not actually feeling very happy with life, so this can't be it.*

Something is missing! "I need to get off this track and find out. I want to know who I am!" I thought to myself.

Soon after, the opportunity presented itself and I found myself in Australia. My partner at the time had been offered a great job opportunity, and I decided to put my career on the back-burner so that I could go and find *myself*. Stripped from the title and esteem I was held in before, I would drive out to Whoop Whoop, as a liquor sales representative, selling and promoting grog to downtrodden bars and pubs.

I was in a new country. I could hardly understand the Australian accent, feeling like a complete alien. The stench of cigarettes and beer, mixed with adrenaline and urine at the RSL clubs at 10 a.m., and the entranced pensioners putting coin after coin in a slot machine, made me physically sick to the bone. I instantly knew that this was no longer for me. I could no longer justify myself returning to a leadership position in this industry, promoting and glamorizing alcoholic beverages, while there were obviously many people lacking the self-regulation skills required to *enjoy in moderation*; one of the industry's catch phrases.

I was desperate to find purpose and meaning in life, and so I went back to healing and steered my career into corporate training and development. Yet, while I was busy helping other people find meaning and purpose, and using their work as a vehicle to achieve so, I had not yet found mine. I would retreat into my inner world, where I would feel connected and at peace, yet my outer world was chaotic and things started to unravel and fall apart.

The two were separate. The connection: Lost. I had shattered the illusion of who I thought I was before, to a point where I could only see greatness in everyone around me, yet I felt small and insignificant. The thought of my *old identity* filled me with shame and embarrassment, and I was floating in a sea of change, not yet knowing who I was or who I was meant to become. And as things started spiralling downwards even more, losing my health, relationship, and work, I came to a fork in the road.

It was at this low point that I had another insight.

We are all a spark from the dazzling light of consciousness. As soon as we leave our spiritual home to enter this world, we are programmed to return and find our way home again. The path of healing from this affliction called *life on Earth* and returning to our magnificent self is not achieved by looking out and up. It is achieved by fully embracing the muddiest, darkest, and most painful places within ourselves; to enter these places with full consciousness and awareness, and then shine and strengthen that little spark of light still left in us.

Unless we enter with conscious choice, effort, and dedication, we risk getting lost in the darkness, identifying with it, and forgetting our true nature. Alternatively, if we only identify with the light, we dissociate from our body and we live life as if in a haze or a dream state.

Our senses are dull. We move through life in a trance, quietly wishing for it to be all over soon to escape this prison and go home to that place where we experience the oneness I remembered so well from my childhood.

It was time to roll up the sleeves, and to embrace life, work, and relationships like I never had before. Every day brought a new opportunity to learn and to give, no matter how small or insignificant. My philosophy of life became very simple: to embrace life and find happiness in every present moment. To slow down and be more patient, let life unfold and guide me for a change.

In the ten years that followed, I found true love and have been blessed with a happy marriage and three beautiful children. I've been able to make choices to balance family and work, and follow my passions for yoga, nutritional medicine, and leadership coaching. I have been able to make peace with my big ego from the past, and have welcomed all the good bits back into my life. It took me a while to figure out that the ego, or lower mind, is actually a great instrument. If you fine tune it to an extent that it becomes an amplifier of magnificence, great things are possible!

Just remember to put it straight back into its box when it starts to claim the credit.

As for the purpose of life, it is to manifest the magnificence, the reverent being inside all of us. We all know this in our heart to be the truth, whatever our own language for magnificence may be. Not expressing it causes disconnect, stress, and illness. Thus, life is a journey of healing and of letting go of beliefs, thoughts, and behaviors that restrict us in our unique expression of our internal magnificence.

About the Author

With her business reSPARK International, Petra Hooijenga inspires small business owners with big dreams to move from stress management to peak performance in business, health, relationships, and life. Having herself been a small business owner for many years, Petra is acutely aware of the stress and challenges facing businesses today, and skillfully assists business owners around the world in navigating a path towards their goals, dreams, and magnificent self in business and life.

Petra holds a bachelor of business administration degree from Nijenrode University in The Netherlands, and is a graduate and member of The Coaching Institute in Melbourne.

Petra lives with her husband and three children in Sydney, Australia.

http://www.respark.com.au

DO I HAVE THE RIGHT TO BE ME?

Carina Jean Lyall

Sitting here writing these words hasn't been an easy process. Getting to the verge of frustration, knowing that I have a story to tell but not really getting it on paper, I left my computer and went to a dinner-party that I had agreed to join.

In that particular group I had always felt a bit strange and out of place. You know the situation where people don't hear half of what you say, laugh at the jokes you make, or ask any questions about the things you say? Well, that night wasn't that much different. I just felt awkward and this well-known feeling started to settle in my stomach.

Walking home later that evening, the feeling had really grown in my system, even though the food had been amazing and there had been a few laughs.

I woke up the next morning feeling blue and had trouble getting up to speed. I meditated for a while and went to a gym class. And all of a sudden, it hit me: the theme of all the stories I had tried to write had created similar sensations in my body and thought patterns.

Each of the stories I had written for this book contained a version of feeling totally wrong or unworthy. In some cases it took the form of guilt; in others, anger or depression. But overall I had felt like I wasn't really good enough just the way I was.

Being a very sensitive person living on this planet, situations tended to overwhelm me. Everything was taken in. The news was like a hor-ror movie and it still is hard for me to let go of other people's suf-fering. Without a filter, navigating around in the impressions, sig-nals, and pain of others can be quite a challenge. People have always referred to me as being very dramatic. I cried too much, laughed too loud, had too hard of a time letting things go, etc. As long as I can remember I wondered why I couldn't be as cool and as easygoing as everyone else.

In today's society we have been blessed with a heightened awareness in regards to personal growth and transformation. We have books, courses, DVDs, teachings by the thousands of different beliefs and directions, most of which claim to have *the* answer to make your pain and suffering go away.

I have been around in a broad selection of these offers, hoping to make me more like everyone else and most of it has been outside myself. Trying to integrate all sorts into my system – a system that didn't really know what it was trying to change – all I knew was that something felt off. With good intentions wanting to improve my life, aiming for a different me, mostly left me with a stronger feeling of not being good enough the way I was, because I just couldn't stick with the programs, didn't understand them, or they just didn't work well with the circumstances I was living in.

The constant search made me go around with my shit in a bag, hoping that someone would take it and throw it away. I was like a blind women fumbling around on the highway.

When I became a mother for the first time, it was like fuel on that fire inside me. With my daughter, love was born. But right after, fear was born as well: knowing that like any other life, this one was just as fragile. Then what I interpreted as guilt entered the room. Guilty that I didn't feel love wash in over me the minute she came out of my uterus. Guilty that I wasn't able to breastfeed her and provide her with the food I was created to give. Guilty that I was so tired, I just wanted to sleep and get away from everything at times. Guilty that I looked like a greaseball and gained too much weight, I wasn't sexy for my partner anymore.

Countless times I have sat on the floor in my daughter's room with a doll, with the little one looking at me waiting for me to start some brilliant scene, but the cat constantly got my tongue. I tried to get her to tell me what to do, but she was so over me. With the sum of that, how could I handle the responsibility of being someone's mother?

Why couldn't I just be like other mothers who had all the right cards on hand, and looked great as well?

It never occurred to me that I could question that standard. But I felt wrong in comparison with something or someone that still hasn't been truly identified to this day. So who sets the bar? Who is it we compare ourselves with? I don't know if it's a lost child inside, acting out the same story over and over again, or if it's that we put up our facades so we don't show the true reality of our lives. Do we lack a collective honesty in the world?

All I can say is that gone without much attention, the sense of wrongness can be an incredible force.

I teach meditation classes for a living. I look around me and see other teachers who look so harmonious and balanced and who are always smiling gently. They tell stories of lives in happiness and ease. I, on the other hand, sit in front of a class and sometimes let out the f-word. I get fed up and yell at my partner and do not feel compassion for every person I meet along the way, some are just *really* annoying. I do not feel the need to go to India and learn from gurus, mostly because I don't like too many people around me.

Yet again I feel I should be different.

I should be more this or that, and how can I sit there and teach anything when it does not meet the standard of other teachers? Others speak of watching every butterfly that flies by and see the beauty in that little miracle. Instead I eyeball cute guys waiting for the bus, enjoying a flirt, caught up in wanting to be seen. Why can't I just be like the others who seem so detached from all of that?

Wrongness as a sensation builds up inside me all the time, but in the past I failed to ask, "Do I have the right to be the way I am, with all that I contain?"

I just assumed the answer was no.

We are bombarded with ways to improve, but is that really possible without first accepting what *is*?

I truly believe that healing the sense of *wrongness* we can feel needs a bit of attention. There can be valuable insights to discover what you already are. However painful that can be at times, there is a true tenderness in letting your being be heard or seen, with compassion instead of a frown.

A turning point for me was when my teacher asked me to stop my jabbering and feel how the sense of not being right showed itself. *How did it move? What did it say? How did it make me feel?* I was forced to stop, breathe with it, and take the bungy jump into my soul. I stood there hooked up to the rope for a long time, not having the courage to jump.

When I did jump, certain things dissolved. I saw my mind on auto-pilot, making up stories on how others live and do things. I saw the stories created on how other people are thinking and pointing their fingers. I saw that the standard I was measuring myself next to... wasn't actually there. But most importantly, for a moment in time, I was meeting all of this with true compassion and patience, knowing that I will slip again at times and feel myself less than enough. I also felt myself being there just the way I am, and that my life was being lived, whether I decided to be fully present or go off boosting my ego in some fairyland where everyone looks like they have been touched by an angel.

I believe that the road to ease and healing is through gentle and compassionate awareness with what arises in our mind body and soul. That peace in us happens when we practice acceptance and letting be.

In my life I have tried to ease and heal pain in my life while searching outside of myself. But how can you possibly act from a place where you are not? You must be where you are to truly take a step forward. It *is* hard work and we may have to accept that life, although brief, cannot be cured with quick fixes, and that the beauty of it is that it is constantly lived. We can't pause it till we get to the good bits. We can learn from the pain by seeing it, accepting it, and treating ourselves with kindness.

By acknowledging our stories and experiences along the way, we can also practice being here right now; letting ourselves be content with what *is*. We can allow ourselves the right to be exactly the way we are.

I may not have a lot of good advice, or ten ways to make your life better. All I have to give you is my honesty, and thoughts on how it has been possible to heal in my life, and I do hope you will take this as some food for thought, inspiration, and something to reflect upon.

About the Author

Carina Jean Lyall is a Dane/Canadian meditation teacher living in Copenhagen, Denmark. Carina was born and raised in Northern Canada and moved to Denmark with her family in 1990. She has worked and lived around the world. What turned her to meditation as a practice was dealing with the effect of working in Bosnia and Kosovo with American and British soldiers; a time that left her with years of anxiety and depression after returning home.

The mother of one, with a second child on the way, Carina blogs and writes for various health blogs in Denmark. Her passion is everyday life and helping people deal with their high pressured lives, huge expectations, and demands.

Hoping that we will become better at treating ourselves with compassion and care is her goal.

http://www.mindfulground.dk/en

AWAKENING CONSCIOUSNESS IN THE TISSUE

Megan Jensen

"You're not going to fall. I won't let that happen," I said. I was sitting in my scrubs at the edge of a hospital bed trying to convince an amputee patient to stand with me.

I graduated with a degree in physical therapy and was working at a job I loved: in the Acute Care Facility at the local hospital. I was good at my job. I enjoyed going to work every day, and with my western medical training and experience, I was sure I had it all figured out. With a passion for healing and blinding optimism, I was often given the patients who refused physical therapy, so that I could convince them to accomplish what they needed in order for them to return home safely.

One day, I came to my last patient of the day. She was wracked with fear.

They had amputated her left leg, and she couldn't bring herself to try standing without it. Sitting at the edge of the hospital bed with a walker in front of us, I had explained to her over and over again that she would use the walker to help her stand up; that I would hold on to her and that, yes, she could do this. I held her hand and made the promise...

"You're not going to fall. I won't let that happen."

Reluctantly, she agreed to try.

"We are going to stand up and sit back down. Just three times," I told her. "Are you ready?"

She nodded and began slowly but surely. She stood, and lowered herself back down to sit on the bed. With the second attempt to stand, she got a little more confident. As she stood up tall for the third and final time, she looked down at her left leg and panicked. Overcome with fear, she flew backwards, pushing the hospital bed just far enough away that it would no longer catch her. My body twisted as I was holding up the flailing 250-pound woman.

My training told me to lower her safely to the floor while my battling intuition screamed, "You made a promise. You better keep her up!"

I managed to call out to the nurses, "I need help in room 244!" as the searing pain shot through my spine. I had kept my promise: the patient had not fallen. But, in the process, I had herniated two discs in my spine.

And I was out of work for weeks.

Lying there on my couch, I convinced myself, "You know how to heal this. You teach others to get well. Just do it yourself."

With renewed determination to heal, I did everything I knew to silence the throbbing pain in my spine. I got my body-fat down to 8%. I began practicing Pilates to strengthen my core. I used hot packs several times a day. I performed every therapeutic stretch I know. But to no avail. Month after month, I was still in pain.

At the end of one of my longer work days, I came home to get the mail and to prepare dinner. The nagging pain in my lower back was beginning to spread out and down my leg, but it had to wait. I sorted through the mail and saw a flyer for a course about connective tissue in the pelvis. I looked down and thought about the deep scar that ran across my belly from a kidney surgery I'd had as a child. It was as if bells were going off and flags were waving. I felt like my formal training had given me very little insight into the pelvis, and yet something told me the answer to my pain could be found there.

A few weeks later, I walked into a seminar filled with physical therapists, nurses, massage therapists and healers. Something was different. The attitude was different; more open. The instructor took the stage. She was a tiny woman, but she was strong. She was muscular from head to toe, and she had an approachable, but assertive, posture.

I felt a connection to her immediately. This woman was a fighter and if anyone could have helped me fight this battle with pain, it would have been her.

I listened intently.

She began instructing about the body as a whole; how you cannot heal one part unless the entire body is in alignment. I loved what I was hearing! We learned several techniques, practiced on each other, and shared the results.

By midday, I realized I didn't have any back pain. Something was changing. I felt looser, somehow.

After lunch, our instructor began teaching a Psoas release. Just by listening to her description of the technique, my body began to shake. I was anxious and sweaty. What was happening to me? My intuition shouted, "This is it!" But I was so scared. How could the answer to my pain be coupled with such fear?

Pairing up, I lied on the table, and allowed my partner to begin the technique. I felt like I was floating above my body, looking down at this girl on the table. She was crying! She must have been in pain! And in a flash, I realized it was me: I was that girl. I was the one crying! In my family, we don't cry; we are strong; we are German. We don't discuss emotions, and we certainly don't show it in a room full of strangers!

I heard the instructor whisper in my ear, "Do you know why you're crying?"

I did. I nodded.

"Allow yourself to fully feel it. It's okay to *feel*. Come all the way back into your body now. It's safe."

The compassion and the love oozing out of this woman struck me. How could she be so strong yet so compassionate at the same time? I listened to what she said. I allowed myself to feel all of the pain, all of the fear, and all of the anger.

I let go.

I felt my muscles release. And when I opened my eyes, I returned back to my seat a changed woman: I was open, alive, and, at least for that moment, pain-free.

After that class, I read all I could about connective tissue. I stumbled upon a sentence that hit me like a ton of bricks: "Repressed emotion is stored in the connective tissue, turning it from a fluid, elastic structure, into a block of concrete, exerting pressure on every muscle, bone, organ, or nerve it surrounds, down to a cellular level".

Freeing emotion could heal pain! That was the answer!

For the next several years I took every class I could on connective tissue, Chinese medicine, kinesiology, and energy.

We are all energy! At our most basic, but most profound level, we are all the same! The answer to true and lasting pain relief is in releasing all of the barriers to energy flow in our bodies. Our consciousness lies in our connective tissue!

I went on to get intensive treatment, and as the tissue released, so did the emotion. Treatments were filled with waves of fear, of nausea, of pain, and tears. As the tissue freed, I gave myself permission to really connect with my emotions, and to just *be myself*. As the daughter of a minister, I had learned that fornicators would be punished by God. As the tissue around my bladder and pelvis released, I remembered being a little girl, and having a doctor examine me while I was ill. I remembered thinking, "If I let him touch me, God will punish me!" And yet my mother was telling me to let him examine me. So my subconscious belief was that my mother wanted me to be punished, and if my own mother and God couldn't love me, I felt as though I must have been worthless.

The feeling of being worthless reflected on my conscious level. Throughout my childhood, high school, and college, I believed I was unlovable and worthless, but never understood why I strongly felt that way. My parents made certain my sister and I had everything we needed. I had friends and I did well in school, yet, many days, I would just sit in front of the mirror and cry from the belief that I was too ugly; too worthless to leave the house.

As my tissue released, the memories surfaced. I remembered being that four year-old girl who rationalized that belief must be true. I understood how she had come to believe it. I felt her sadness, her desperation, and her anxiety, as if I were feeling it again in that very moment. Except with that new understanding, I now had the ability to tell my four year-old self what the doctor was doing was okay. He was trying to help me. My mother had only wanted to stop me from being sick. With that awareness, I chose to fully connect with my emotions of such a situation, and I let go. I understood that I could free myself of the belief of being worthless and unlovable; that that I could build on my self-esteem; that I could make peace with my mother, and with God.

Little by little, subconscious beliefs surfaced; fear of being punished by God; fear of not being good enough; fear of losing my family and friends; fear of being alone; fear of being in a loveless marriage. Little by little, I saw the moment I chose to accept each belief and I chose to release each one in that moment of the treatment.

I had also learned that the Universe hates a void, so as I freed myself of negative beliefs and memories, and remained open to love and light, wonderful people came into my life. I found supportive relationships with unconditional love. As my emotional-being healed, my physical-being did too. My depression lifted, I never felt that back pain again, and as I was able to stand in my truth, I was able to love myself.

Now with a renewed spirit, and a healthy body, I began to use these same techniques to treat patients. Time and again, I saw that as their tissue released, their emotions did too. To my surprise, I realized the inverse was also true. A patient who can first release the emotion will experience the tissue-releasing response. We have the power to choose how we begin to heal, through the mind, or through the body. But either way, the spirit is renewed and energy flows more freely.

The most beautiful thing I have learned in treating patients over the last ten years is that no two people have the same injury. I might see twenty patients a week with back pain, but they will all require a different path to healing. We all have different emotional barriers, traumas, allergies, environmental stresses, fears, passions, relationships, diets, and all of that plays a part in our physical, emotional, and spiritual well-being. As long as we're looking at the patient's symptoms, and not the person as a whole, we are missing our opportunity to restore true and complete balance to their energy system.

With balance, any person can heal themselves. I continue to work one on one with patients to help them find their spirit, listen to their intuition, open to fully feeling the pain they've experienced, and to give themselves permission to let it go. With each patient I treat, I heal another part of myself. With that transfer of energy, we as a unit become closer to the whole; closer to the pure existence of love, which is what heals all things.

About the Author

Megan Jensen is a board certified holistic health practitioner. She graduated with a degree in physical therapy from Fairleigh Dickenson University in 2001, and practiced in a hospital setting until an injury in 2005 led her on her own healing journey.

After receiving only temporary relief from traditional rehabilitation, she began studying alternative medicine in 2006. Megan found an effective combination of myofascial release, bioenergetic kinesiology, and health counseling that she uses to help her patients along the road to recovery. She combines this approach with an understanding of Eastern medicine and culture.

Most recently, Megan graduated from the Institute for Integrative Nutrition to ensure she is providing her patients with a holistic approach to achieving a healthy mind, body, and spirit. Her goal is to help each patient find a personalized treatment approach that will return them to pain-free, active motion.

http://www.lendahandtherapy.com

THE INNER JOURNEY TO HAPPINESS

Frank Boffa

In early 2012, something profound happened to me.

After being on an inner journey of transformation for ten years, a distinct change in my reality had taken place. I had stepped into a base level of happiness that I had experienced glimpses of over the years, but never dreamed possible as a state of being that I felt anchored in.

What was extraordinary about my heightened level of happiness was that it was not dependent on anything external in my life. There were certainly no particular events that had occurred in early 2012 to make me so happy all of a sudden. *This happiness simply emanated from within.*

I found myself waking up day after day, feeling excited about life, for no apparent reason. Simple things, like the experience of feeling the breeze on my face would trigger states of blissful appreciation for life. My heart had opened immensely to my fellow human beings and I would even find myself feeling love for complete strangers, seeing them as beautiful souls on their journey of life. I would sit in awe of the beauty in nature and I could feel the Divine essence in everyone and everything.

Life also seemed to be returning this new level of happiness and love to me. Everyone I interacted with seemed more open-hearted. People I passed on the street would smile.

Suddenly, the whole world was smiling at me.

Of course, my new state of higher happiness did not make me immune to being *human* and feeling heavy emotions. But my experience of these emotions had changed. I found that I experienced heavy emotions from a space of being anchored in my higher level of happiness. I was able to observe these emotions without being drawn into them. They would then pass quickly, without too much disturbance to my harmonious state of being.

Life had changed... big time! A dramatic shift in my state of being had taken place. *But what had happened? How did this happen?*

I began my inner journey of healing ten years prior to this. At that time, my reality was very different to the state of being that I have described. I was working in a profession that, although paid well, did not provide me with a sense of fulfillment and felt far removed from who I really was. My life was devoid of passion and purpose, and I found myself often immersed in heavy emotional states.

I had no clarity as to what it was that would bring a sense of purpose and fulfillment to my life. I didn't know what I was passionate about; I didn't know who I was; I felt frustrated and stuck in this heavy, unfulfilling place.

My heart was calling for something to change. I finally took action by reducing my work to part-time in order to create some space to explore what it was that would make me feel excited about life... something... anything that would ignite some degree of passion within.

I embarked upon this search with great enthusiasm, enrolling in various courses and dabbling in different fields of work. I was enjoying new experiences, but hadn't discovered quite what it was that made my heart sing. Despite feeling disillusioned at times, something urged me to move forward in my exploration.

Somehow, this search one day, led me to explore the study of energy healing as a potential, alternative field of work. I naively thought that I would simply learn about the concepts of working with energy to assist the healing of disorders in the physical body. I had no idea that I was about to embark on an extraordinary inner journey that would dramatically change my life.

I now understood how it worked. Everything in my outer reality was a reflection of that which I held within. By taking complete responsibility for creating my life as it currently was, I was able to access my power to re-create it; to create something different.

I learnt that when events occur in life that are held unresolved, a holding of energies within takes place, distorting our perceptions of life, our perceptions of our self and creating us to live unconsciously in patterns of behavior that do not serve us. Also, some of these energies are inherited from our family's genetic lines, energies from the unresolved experiences of our parents and ancestors, all passed down to us genetically and impacting how we live our life.

These energies, I learnt, are also the basis of physical illness manifesting in the body.

What was very clear to me now was that my search to discover my passions and purpose and to find greater fulfillment in life needed to be directed within. I realized that I had a lot of work to do! But also, most remarkably, I had found something that ignited a great passion within me.

My inner journey had begun. I was learning how to become conscious of, and meet, the energies that I held within, which had created my life to be as it was.

As I uncovered and released layers of old, stored energy, something new would come in; a greater connection to my higher consciousness and greater access to gifts that had been dormant. Life was changing.

I was changing.

The more I proceeded on this inner journey, the more accelerated it became and I found myself increasingly being led by an inner guidance that would direct me to my highest path and choices in life. Sometimes it took a great amount of trust to follow that which came simply as a clear knowing from within. Following this inner knowing has always proved the highest choice, despite the mind struggling at times to understand the logic behind a directed course of action.

One day, I felt drawn to pick up a paintbrush and start painting. Despite not having any training in painting, I was led by this inner guidance to utilize creativity as a means of transforming and releasing energies that I held within. I discovered that by putting the mind aside, connecting with my body and emotions and painting from this state of inner connection, the release of stored energies onto the canvas took place.

Painting became a big part of my journey of transformation and I often sat in front of the canvas in awe of the release process that had just taken place and the new insights that would then come in. The paintings themselves radiated energy and seemed to be an energetic imprint of what had occurred in the process of creating them. Simply looking at them would then trigger more of the same energy held within me to surface for release.

A whole new reality was opening up for me; a magical journey that guided me to connect with gifted healers, teachers, and highly evolved beings in many parts of the world.

I discovered the beauty of how unique this journey is for each of us. I discovered that there is no *one way* of embarking upon it other than simply following the pulsing of one's own inner truth; *following this inner truth always.*

This journey has been extraordinarily rewarding as well as immensely challenging at times. It has taken me to places of meeting the deepest pain held within my being.

The inner journey of healing and transformation is a journey of great courage. It requires courage to let go of old beliefs and identities that have formed one's very foundation in life and courage to follow the inner calling that drives one forward on this journey, despite those around you simply not getting it. It requires courage to meet the pain held within.

At various points I have certainly cried, "Enough! I want to get off this ride now, it is far too challenging. Life was so much easier when I was sleepwalking through life."

It is certainly easier to choose not to embark on this journey, to skirt around, and to suppress the pain held within rather than meeting it head on. But then life is also rather dull and unfulfilling in comparison.

The most challenging period that I encountered on this journey began in early 2011, one year prior to the experience of stepping into my new base level of happiness. At this time, two challenging events occurred in my life simultaneously, namely the ending of a long-term relationship and the death of my father.

These events, whilst met with great acceptance, were a catalyst for a profound inner process of transformation. Old, stored energies were being triggered for release in a way that I had never before experienced with such a high degree of intensity.

During this intensely challenging period, I was forced to keep my energy focused on my inner world. I was physically exhausted and could only put minimal energy into my outer world to keep things flowing. I had limited interaction with friends and spent much time connecting with nature.

This process continued for a period of one year and as it neared completion, I found that moments of happiness would begin finding their way in amongst the intense heaviness of old energies that were clearing. Something extraordinary was occurring within. And in a way, it was a completion of all that I had been working on, meeting and releasing for the past ten years since my magical, inner journey had begun.

What resulted from this, the astounding leap into greater happiness and higher consciousness when this intense period came to completion, had certainly made the past ten years feel very worthwhile.

Of course, there is always more; more growth, happiness, fulfillment, and higher consciousness to be accessed. And though it feels that I have arrived somewhere wonderful, the journey always continues.

I have learnt, both from my own journey and through participating in that of others, that the journey of healing begins with the courage to meet the pain that is stored within; discovering how to transform this pain with the power of your open heart; meeting it all with love, accepting all, forgiving all, taking responsibility for creating, and holding it all, and ultimately surrendering it all to a higher part of your being. Letting it go with love.

For love is always the key: this great force that brings resolution to the deepest of pain.

With this comes the stepping into higher consciousness and greater happiness; the claiming of the profound gifts that lie hidden within all that we experience as painful and challenging.

In all of this, you are you are rebuilding your connection within. It is a connection to a higher part of your being that is beyond your physical, mental, and emotional reality. It is a connection to a part of you that some may call your higher self or the Divine essence that resides within all.

This is the source of your true happiness – a happiness that emanates from within – regardless of what occurs in your outer life.

All with whom you interact with in life, whether for a short or long period of time, are here to assist you on this great journey of reconnection to this inner source of fulfillment, regardless of what is triggered for you in these interactions. How then could you *not* love and appreciate them all?

I set out on this journey to find something. I was searching for happiness, fulfillment, passion, and purpose; words that I have used to describe that which I was seeking from my external reality. I was led instead to a place within. A place that I discovered is the Source of all that we endlessly search for in our outer world. This place is a part of you and the experience of meeting this part within... that is indeed beyond any of these words.

About the Author

From Sydney, Frank Boffa enjoys engaging in his many passions in life including the creation of artwork, writing, and music from a state of inner connection.

His greatest passion involves playing a role in the inner journey of transformation for others... the journey of awakening to one's highest, true self.

Frank utilizes his gifts as a healer and teacher to support this journey to take place for others in an accelerated and graceful way. He feels strongly about doing this work in a way that is empowering for others, directing them always back to their own inner source of guidance and truth.

Frank conducts both personal sessions and group work and derives much joy from teaching others through the programs he has developed. His work facilitates a shift into a higher consciousness, the release of old patterns of being, and the connection to one's inner source of fulfillment and happiness.

http://www.frankboffa.com

IT IS A GOOD DAY TO DIE

Jennifer T. Cornell, M.D.

He lay in a coma. The corners of his bed were draped with tobacco-filled pouches in the color of the four directions: red for the east, yellow for the south, black for the west and white for the north. There were eagle feathers everywhere, sweet grass bundles, and sage burning. But why was he in a coma?

The medical reasons were obvious to me. He has brain metastasis from his bowel cancer that had first made him confused, and now these brain lesions had swollen, causing him to slip into a coma. The question still lingered: Why had he chosen this rather than death?

This may be a strange question for his doctor to be asking, but this was neither an ordinary patient nor an ordinary doctor-patient relationship.

When I graduated from my residency in Family Practice I chose to work on a Native American Reservation in northern Minnesota. We had a five-doctor practice and a nine-bed hospital with a dialysis unit. It was a big shock to work here coming out of training, as the level of care we provided in this remote hospital was high. It was not unusual to have cardiac arrest and car accidents. Near the end of my time there, I even treated some gunshot wounds. But when I arrived I was still a wide-eyed new graduate that wanted to make a difference in the world.

But I have diverged from the real story here: Bob in his coma.

Bob was a patient of another doctor when I came to the reservation and was already diagnosed with bowel cancer. The cancer could have been prevented, however he had chosen not to have the surgery that could have helped him. I never asked him why he made this choice. It was a mute point by the time I became his doctor.

Bob knew he was dying. He was facing it with grace and dignity.

Near the end of his life, he decided to change doctors and work with me. Again I never asked him why but assumed it to be because his doctor was part of the Native American Church he attended. I was also aware that Bob knew *I needed him* as a patient. I was disillusioned with the place and was looking for the connections I had found on the Navajo Reservation where I worked as a medical student. There was a soul on the Navajo Reservation that I was not finding on the Ojibwa. Bob offered me hope of finding that again. Somehow he knew that offering himself as my patient allowed me in a way to connect to the soul that did exist there.

Up until that point it had seemed hopeless. I was delivering teenage mothers (some of them their second baby) and was seeing alcoholism and drug abuse. My successes were limited at times to just helping one girl not get pregnant. Here, despite working with amazing doctors and some wonderful patients, I was not finding the spiritual connection I had found with the Navajo people, where I had worked with medicine men and healers.

So Bob became my patient. He was still young, in his fifties, yet nearing the end of his life. Born into a religious family, he was destined to become an Episcopalian Minister till he chose another path. His path took him to the Souix Reservation where he was adopted by the Lakota and found his native roots. There he became a sun dancer and danced in this sacred tradition. Later he embraced his own tribe's tradition and became a Midewiwin: an Ojibwa medicine man.

When I met him he had become a member of the Native American Church. He also danced *powwow* and was a whistle-carrier. This honor, passed on from one person to the next, gave the whistle-carrier the duty of working with the drummers and to whistle up a drum that was playing well, or a particular song to keep the energy of the *powwow* moving. He was a traditional dancer, which meant he took on the persona of an animal and danced by imitating its movements, with a bustle of eagle feathers on his head and back (these dances are quite spellbinding to watch)

Through working with Bob, it became clear that he had decided to integrate his life in his death. He talked with me about his hopes and plans, and when he was hospitalized for pain control we spent time together planning his wake and funeral. This was how I spent my night shifts when not busy in our little emergency room. Bob wanted to make his death meaningful by bringing together all the traditions with which he had been involved. He hoped to bring the spirit of them all to one place: his wake and funeral. Through allowing me to help him with this, he brought me closer to the soul of the Ojibwa people. He also spent time working on reconciling as much of his life as he could, and tried to clear some of the skeletons out of his closet.

When Bob was nearing the end of his life he was hospitalized again for pain control. The Veterans Day *powwow* was approaching and he was one of the people being honored. A veteran of three wars, Bob asked if I would help him attend the *powwow* knowing well that I was an avid spectator, and later a dancer.

So Bob, his girlfriend, and I ended up sitting on the wooden bleachers watching the event. In November the powwows are held indoors to escape the snowy weather. There were four drum groups in the space, as was the custom. I sat with him and injected him with morphine so he could withstand the pain of sitting.

At this point I did not know that he was a whistle-carrier, as he had it under his shirt. He got up suddenly during a war song and went to stand behind the drum that was playing. This was a great effort for him. He whistled up the song, meaning they were to play four more sets. He stood behind the drum, dancing in place the best he could. When the drum stopped, the room fell silent and Bob announced that this was his last dance, and that he would soon be choosing who would next carry his whistle.

The silence was piercing.

Later he again went out onto the floor with the other veterans, where he was honored by being given an eagle feather. In the US, only native people are allowed to collect and own eagle feathers. These are used in *powwows* and in healing and are given as a great honor. Bob returned to the stand and handed the eagle feather to me.

I was floored.

With tears in my eyes he said that I had earned it; that I had made all this possible.

I had learned from Bob how to have a good death. Bob showed me how not to be afraid of death but to rather embrace and savor it. He embodied this for me. He also showed me that it was not always about making a difference but about being present and listening. It was not so much about the *doing* as the *being*. How was I showing up for patients? Was I busy trying to make a difference or was I truly listening to what was important in their lives?

So Bob's funeral was written, his wake planned, and he had cleared as many skeletons in his closet as he could. He was ready to face death. He had decided everything: his pall bearers; his honor songs; who would speak at his grave side; and where he would be buried.

Bob was ready. However, he then developed the brain metastasis and became confused. We all knew he was close to death so said our good byes.

And then Bob lapsed into a coma.

Day after day he laid there. Why was he lingering if he was so ready to go to the happy hunting ground? It was thought that it was because he had not finished the bustle-eagle feather worn for *powwow*, so someone finished it and hung it in his room. The room was so thick with eagle feathers and sage smoke that it felt like a holy place.

But still… he lingered.

Next, his girlfriend received a call from a medicine man in southern Minnesota. He had seen Bob in a dream leaving his body, but then turning around and following his footsteps back to his body. So the medicine man asked her if he had his moccasins on. In their tradition, the moccasins are to be placed on the wrong feet so the soul could not follow the foot prints back to the body. Bob's girlfriend drove to his home and back (a two-hour drive) to get his moccasins. It was a night I was on call so I was in the hospital. She placed the moccasins on the wrong feet and then left to get some ribbon to tie them on with. It was then that Bob finally left us.

He had planned it all so well… but we had forgotten the moccasins.

About the Author

Jennifer Cornell is a board certified family and holistic doctor, and a fellow of the Royal Australian College of GPs. She has enjoyed a rich life during her twenty-five years in medicine, including working in private practice, emergency rooms, and in indigenous health.

She has a real passion for indigenous health and worked with more than ten tribes from the bottom of the Grand Canyon to an island in Alaska. Most recently she has spent the last five years with the Maori in New Zealand and then moved to Australia to work in an Aboriginal clinic. Her other passion is alternative medicine, which she had learned from the medicine men and healers of these various tribes. She took this to another level in 2001 when she became board certified in holistic medicine. She has recently fulfilled her dream of starting an integrated clinic where all healing modalities work together to affect change.

http://drjennifertcornell.wordpress.com/

FROM CHRONIC FATIGUE TO HEALTH AND WHOLENESS

Kim Minos

I have always deeply loved nature. It was at school that I would turn essays and writings into pieces about how we as humans are not living in harmony with nature, regardless of the topic that had been set. As a teenager I had been involved with starting an environmental group, wanting to make a difference and getting involved in environmental activism projects to protect areas of great natural beauty and significance. And because I found solace and an acceptance in nature, this was more important to me than the subjects I was studying at school. Nature provided me with a familiarity which I did not understand but did not need to. I just felt my *friends unseen* were in nature, feeling more connection with it than with people.

Later I went through a period of time living like a bit of a hermit, feeling closer to the trees than I did with people. They were easier to communicate with and their responses seemed to make more sense. The presence of sacredness in the experiences of oneness and connectedness in nature were very real and I found this more meaningful than whatever else the rest of life had to offer.

I did not understand what was going on with me and I spent long periods of time staying at home in the bush not going out to see anyone, preferring to be alone and commune with the energies in nature. There were those around me who were becoming concerned about my sanity and lack of balance in life, and there were times where I too was also a little concerned. I was retreating into the forest and learning to live off what I could find growing there, along with whatever was in my garden, which, when winter came, was not a lot.

I had judgments about how humanity was not living a balanced respectful relationship with the natural environment. Little did I realize how these judgments would later reflect in my own life experiences, showing me where I was not living in harmony with my own nature.

In an attempt to correct the apparent imbalances in my life, I ventured out into the world again to find work and relate with people. Having a natural affinity for plants and gardens (I had worked as a landscape gardener while going to university to study engineering), I found I was more fulfilled designing gardens than bridges and roads and so for a time this became my work.

In going back out into the world I buried parts of me that were still in the process of healing, such as unresolved emotional issues from past relationships, pretending to get about in the world as though everything was okay. I had disconnected from what my heart was telling me, forming a relationship that was never going to work, and tried to push on regardless.

And… it did not work. One day I came down with a cold and fever. For six months I could not shake it off and on Christmas Eve I fell into a state that I did not recover from until seven years later. I had developed chronic fatigue syndrome (CFS), fibromyalgia, and multiple allergy-type sensitivities.

I experienced an extreme level of fatigue that I could not have previously imagined. I was in pain through much of my body and I had become allergic to most of what was around in the twentieth century: from plastics, fumes, petrochemicals, chemicals in the food chain, foods, and even the scents and oils from certain plants. This latter part really bothered me. My earlier judgments were coming back to haunt me, but more on that later.

I developed ongoing headaches, I was unable to focus, and was not able to sleep to effectively recover. If I was able to work for an hour or two I would spend the next three or four days recovering. There were days where I could not walk for more than a few minutes, and going to the en-suite bathroom was a major expedition that required recovery time on the floor before I could get back to my bed.

Things were not looking good.

I had been feeling like I needed a change in the direction of my life, and six months prior to becoming ill I had begun to study naturopathy. It was more than a little ironic that soon after I had begun to study about natural health I would become more ill than I could have possibly imagined. I went to doctors, allergy specialists, naturopaths, homoeopaths, psychologists, counselors, and psychiatrists. I was looking at physical, emotional, and psychological approaches and willing to try anything apart from the suggestion of one doctor who suggested antidepressants. I pointed out that if he had felt the way I had for as long as I had, he too would be feeling a little depressed.

I tried nutritional approaches, herbs, supplements, and IV injections of vitamin C which made significant differences to my energy while I was having them. I went through periods of having cold-bath treatments as a process to stimulate the immune system in my body. Some things helped. Others did not. And on good days I was experiencing a reduction in the levels of fatigue.

On one of my journeys I went to see a channel and healer. She gave me the best piece of common sense psychological insight I had ever heard. She said, "You do not know what it is that you are feeling."

I was a bit stunned by this. How could I not *know* what I was feeling? I pondered this and, in doing so, I realized just how much truth what she shared carried. I *could* identify physical experiences and sensations – that, was obvious – but I was *not* so much in touch with my feelings emotionally.

A light dawned. This was the beginning of the return for me. I had spent most of my life feeling what other people wanted and I just responded *thinking* that it was me. There was a clue in the *thinking* bit. One cannot know feelings by thinking about them; feelings are to be felt. Thinking was a step removed from feeling. I had been avoiding and denying my feelings in a number of areas of my life and not had the courage to really face them. This was most apparent in my relationship at that time, where I was not listening to my heart and was staying for all the wrong reasons.

The thing about not listening to the voice in your heart is that when you do it once, it becomes easier to do it again and before long you forget you are doing it at all. So I put my attention on developing a new relationship with myself, deciding it was time to end the avoidance and denial of my feelings. I just wanted to know the truth.

And so my relationship ended.

I realized I had judgments about my feelings and the more I judged them the more baggage I had accumulated. I needed to release the judgments I had of my feelings. As I felt them one by one without judgment, gradually my backlog of unresolved feelings began to release as I let them go with gratitude.

Little by little my energy returned. The nutritional supplements and herbal medicines were helping but, on the days when feelings began to clear, I felt the weight of the illness lifting from me, and in doing so I could feel more and more of what was authentic for me.

My relationships changed. I began to accept and trust my feelings, and the more I did this, the more I trusted and accepted myself. This was a self-loving thing to do: to allow myself to *just feel* my feelings without judging them. Through this I overcame the inertia of my past and was able make new choices in my life. Who I thought I was, was no longer true for me. I was changing and letting go. It was very much a process of un-becoming what I was not.

Gradually, by having the courage of choosing to live from my heart and accepting the truth, my energy returned and the allergies disappeared. I developed a new relationship with my physical and emotional bodies. I began listening to and honoring the inherent intelligences within. Through this, my relationships, work, and health changed.

I grew and I have a new sense of compassion and understanding for how we affect ourselves when we do not listen to our heart and compromise our truth. Life has a way of reflecting back to us all of our choices. The circumstances created from my choices not based in love gave me the opportunity to see that as a creator of my Universe I can co-create different outcomes. With courage we make love-based choices creating joy rather than suffering as the experience for our learning and growth.

Thankfully, it has been many years since I experienced the debilitating effects of CFS, fibromyalgia, and allergies, and I am profoundly grateful for the experience and the learning during this time. Perhaps I could have done this learning differently but this is the way I *chose* to do it. I have fully recovered. Through this experience I gained more wisdom, empathy, and understanding which, through my work in the school of naturopathy and in my practice each day, have been turned into something beneficial for others.

The process of healing has been one of *healing apparent separations* within my self. What I had been judging, avoiding, and denying is being felt and released on an ongoing basis. The healing space that I experienced in nature was one that I needed to hold for myself; the experience of unity and oneness; that we are not separate from anything. I had yet to fully bring it home and feel all of that within myself. We have all of nature within us. We are not separate from any of the other kingdoms, whether mineral, devic, plant, or animal kingdoms, or the kingdom of souls.

Once we fully understand this, there is no way we can continue treating this beautiful planet the way we have been.

About the Author

Kim Minos loves the fields of natural medicine and growth and development. He has worked as a naturopath for sixteen years and during this time He has lectured in naturopathy and developed the naturopathy program for Insight Foundation.

He wrote the Advanced Diploma of Naturopathy to incorporate the principles of *know thy self* so that students undergo their own processes of clearing limitations and fear-based patterns, to develop a strong foundation for when they go out into practice.

Kim loves spending time in the bush and in the garden getting his hands in the dirt growing herbs for medicines and food. He is a mentor in personal and spiritual growth bringing principles of personal spiritual alchemy into practice with practitioners and students.

He also enjoys spending time with his daughter and three grandchildren and hanging out in the cool climate forests.

http://www.holisticwellness.net.au

I AM WHO I CHOOSE TO BE

Debbie Seaton

As I look back at the windy path of my life's journey, the changing winds of time caress my face as the shadows of the past fade into a haze of memories. Life had given me so many opportunities and I shall never forget where I came from. Now, I can smile and breathe a sigh of relief as I face my past with an open heart, knowing that every experience had made me who I am today.

Born in Sydney, I was the eldest of four children. My childhood was rough with constant financial hardship and parents drowning into severe addictions. At such a tender age, life was an emotional rollercoaster, a journey of rejection and abandonment and a struggle to survive.

When I was eight, my parents separated. My mother left to find happiness with another man, and our father was incapable of caring for us. My five year-old brother and I were not wanted; such a wretched and soul-destroying feeling for us both at such a young age. Eventually we went to live with our grandfather and his wife in a totally loveless environment.

I clearly remember my brother and I having a secret place under a bush, where we would sit every day. To this day, this memory is still so vivid. In this secret and safe haven of ours, my brother and I would hold hands sharing stories with each other, dreaming how our Mum was coming back to take us away and love us again.

We eventually went back to live with our mother four years later. There were many memories over the years; the birth and death of a baby sister, who had touched my heart to its very core for three weeks before she left us; my mother and stepfather's alcohol addiction; their emotional and physical abuse. There are many sad and painful accounts from my childhood.

While this may be where I come from, this is not who I am today.

Meeting my husband when I was seventeen years old – a marriage that lasted thirty-four years – gladly helped me escape from a tormented life. It was a joy and I was so grateful to him for a life so far removed from my childhood experiences. Our eldest daughter was born six weeks before we were married; a few days before my twentieth birthday. Over the next four years, a son and a younger daughter joined our lives. We lived in Sydney, Australia for the first eighteen months of our marriage then moved to Bathurst; a large country town in New South Wales.

My fondest memories are that of my children. I smile inside and outside at their wonderful sense of humor and their ability to see the funny side of life. Of course, along the years, my children were faced with trials and tribulations as they grew into their teenage years. Seeing each of their lives as if it were a filmstrip, now that they themselves are married with children of their own, makes me feel so blessed to be their Mum. In the later years of my marriage, my husband and I lived on a beautiful property just outside of Bathurst.

But our marriage was starting to break down at that time. I had taken the path of self-discovery and my husband had not. As I was growing and expanding more, determined to explore who I really was, a gap appeared between us and we grew apart. There were times when we nearly left each other and we would relent and give our marriage another go. This only smoothed our marriage for a short time. Then, it was finally time. We had given it our best and we both decided to move on. We divorced and we both embarked on our own separate journeys as old friends.

I found myself alone starting a new life in Perth, on the other side of Australia, at age fifty-two. Being Australia's width away from my children and grandchildren was challenging. Even though I did have many friends, the feeling of living and being totally alone without the responsibility of another was bizarre. This was a time, an opportunity, to explore and delve deeper into myself. I must say it was quite an experience as I faced the tidal wave of what I had avoided and denied throughout my life. It felt so deep, like many lifetimes joined into one! Even though there was support around me, nothing and no one filled the emptiness of the chasm which I felt inside.

In truth, it was time to face the fear and the illusion of *I can't* beliefs taken on from what I had been told, and what I had created for myself. I felt how I had learned to endure life, to appreciate its good times during the bad ones, while constantly compromising and invalidating myself. My self-esteem was low. I was crippled by fear of rejection. My life was always about others. I had no idea what I wanted or needed.

This was a rough time for me.

My first food-shopping experience on my own was of walking around, close to tears, inside a supermarket because I could not for the life of me work out what I liked to eat. I found myself walking to the checkout with just the bare essentials at the bottom of the trolley. There was also the question of how I was going to make a living. I had hurt myself at work twelve years prior, had two major surgeries, and, to top it off, was told I would never be able to work again, with my employers retiring me on a disability pension from my superfund.

My situation felt grim and confronting. There were several obstacles before me: My age and my disability, and my own beliefs in the boxes, limitations, labels, and systems that society imposed to control how I should look or what I should believe. And I bought into those limitations; I take responsibility for that.

But one day, mustering the courage, I walked into an employment agency.

I was promptly told by a girl, who seemed to be eighteen years old, that I needed to be retrained; that the likelihood of finding a job at my age with a disability from an injury went against me in the workforce. I was referred to a government body and given a case worker who retrained people like me: those in the *too old with a disability* box. I was sent to doctors, assessed, and told I could only work so many hours a week should I ever find a job.

Determined to find a career a few years prior, having completed a certificate IV in community services helped. At least it was a direction. I had also just recently started a course in mentoring and life coaching which also helped. But how was I going to use these skills? What job could I get which required no experience? I pondered it for so long. Then the answer came: financial counsellor! My heart started to sing. I could work with people like myself, being able to give back from my own life experience.

So with hope growing inside of me, I enrolled myself in a diploma of community services, specializing in financial counselling. It was an eighteen-month course and I found myself very busy with two courses to complete. I was feeling the challenge I had given myself. It was a real stretch; always having doubts about my abilities and judging myself as being not very smart. It was a long process, which pushed me beyond the limitations I had imposed upon myself.

Regularly visiting my case worker, who was supposed to be assisting me to get back into the workforce, was depressing. Regardless of how positive my attitude was, it felt like I was being held back and was provided with absolutely no encouragement or belief in my ability to succeed.

Then, why everything felt like such a challenge, hit me hard. I realized that I was caught up in the giant mix of an illusion; that I had to break free from the system; from the *I can't, I am too old* disability box that I had allowed myself to be caught up in. My hope and self-determination started to grow again, really affirming I can succeed.

For part of my training as a financial counsellor, I was placed two days a week volunteering with a financial counselling service. This was a blessing, for I was getting the much needed skills and experience to apply for a financial counselling position.

Finally finishing my certificate IV in a mentoring and life coaching course gave me some confidence to start lifting the lid off the box; the system I was determined to break out of. I became grateful to the case worker I had. Her lack of encouragement and her constant talk of obstacles and hurdles that awaited me had only made my self-determination stronger. I continued my studies with only six months to go and it felt like it was time to take that step up and find a job.

While attending our monthly financial counselling workshop, I overheard that there was a job going. It was full-time and, without hesitation, I decided to give it a go. The next day I sent my resume and to my surprise, within hours they contacted me to come in and look around. I couldn't believe what I saw. Did they ask me to start the job the next day?!

There was but one glitch: the job was only a three-month one and I wasn't allowed to work with the pension I was on. So I had to make a decision: To let the past go, let my pension go, and trust that I would be ok, or risk losing the opportunity of the full-time job. I decided to go for the former. So I rang the case worker and told her of my decision. There was nothing she could say. It was done! I had broken out of the system, moved back into living, and trusted myself. I am still working there after twelve months with the contract consistently being extended.

I have had a full life-experience and have learnt to keep walking forward and not look back with regret. I do not stop for anyone or anything. I create my own reality and my own future. What really amuses me is that the profession I chose as a financial counsellor is what I call 'system busting', meaning that I *can* make a difference. I have learnt to transform my own self-imposed limitations and those that society and the system had put in place to keep me small and controlled. I am highly enjoying life on my journey along the path of self-discovery, ever learning new things. I am unstoppable in stepping into my plan and purpose, exploring within my own self why I am here on this beautiful little planet.

Looking back at my parents, how I grew up and the journey that has brought me to this very moment, I now have so much more understanding of how everyone in my life has done their best through their own life experience. I have learnt that within life there is always a choice: I can either stay in my comfort zone, never take a risk, and slowly but surely die inside, or step out of the box to live a rich life that goes way beyond anything my parents could have dreamed of. Like many, they gave in to what they believed about themselves, never allowing themselves to wonder if they could have been so much more; what they could have been. They never realized that they could have reached for the stars and beyond if only they hadn't identified with the boxes, limitations, and judgments they had allowed themselves believing from everyone; their parents, teachers, peers, religion, and society in general.

"Thanks, Mum. Thanks, Dad. Thanks for showing me how to be more. I understand now, having grown up, that you did the best you could through your own life experience. Many thanks and love for bringing me into this world to learn to love and grow and experience a full life."

About the Author

Debbie Seaton is a financial wellness coach, counselor and mentor, offering advice and knowledge in the area of financial freedom by embracing abundance and success. Known for her ability to discover and clear blocks that prevent people's full potential, Debbie offers classes, mentoring, and coaching that examine every day money issues from a practical level while using the universal principals of abundance to expand one's life.

Currently working as a financial counselor, Debbie is an active community advocate for financial accountability and encourages all to take control of their lives through responsible actions. Debbie holds a diploma in financial counselling, a Certificate IV in coaching and mentoring, and a Certificate IV in training and education.

http://www.aspiritualbudget.com

AMIDST CHAOS, THE WOMAN DANCED

Michelle Renee' Bernardo

As a young girl, I always knew in my heart I would someday live in New York City. In my mind, this was the capital of the world. There was something I experienced each time I went to this city that gave me the aspirations to become an artist; a dreamer of dreams; it empowered me with hope.

After obtaining my associates degree in Illustration and graphic design and a four-year college degree in art education, I landed my first job in New York's East Village as a visual merchandizing manager in a house and garden department store. The company eventually went out of business, and there I was living in an all-girl's residential hotel in Manhattan, with no job.

I have always been a spiritually-attuned, intuitive person who looks internally for answers and guidance through quiet contemplation. I felt a tug at my heart to become a floral designer and entrepreneur, with the goal of eventually owning a flower shop in the city.

With a brain thirsty for knowledge, I attended a floral design school and went to New York University's school of business for certificate programs. With creativity running in my veins, I found myself working full-time for the busiest flower shop on 14th Street and Fifth Avenue in New York. I was even able to join a gym across the street where I would work out for two hours to decompress from the day's activities.

As a child, the impetus to sign up for real estate school had also been a soul calling. I remember reading the classified section of the Sunday paper with great interest, decoding abbreviations such as '3BR' and '2BR with FP,' with tremendous enthusiasm.

After running into a friend from college who was a New York City real estate agent, I knew this was something that would afford me with better financial independence.

I have always had terrific beginner's luck, like pitching a no-hitter for my softball team, my first time on the mound! The first week working as a rental agent I rented five apartments. I clicked my heels and off I went, but this ego driven situation did not go as well as planned, and I soon became discouraged.

By that time, I was finding my sleep off-kilter, and my three-year relationship was beginning to suffer due to my partner's excessive drinking. I found myself devouring Advil like candy. Sleep issues, difficulty finding my footing, and lack of concentration were noticeably affecting my reality. Other than running, sitting in silence, reading scripture from the bible, or looking at puppies in the store-window below my apartment, few things tapped the pleasure center of my brain.

I had been living in the city for seven years, keeping my own apartment; however, finances forced me to move in with my girlfriend. Her drinking worsened, and though she bought me a puppy to keep me company while she stayed after work to drink with the guys from Wall Street, my behavior entered bizarre mode. I would wake in the middle of the night hearing the sound of ocean waves in my head. I would climb to the upstairs loft to curl-up in a ball and cry myself to sleep. I missed having my own apartment.

My younger brother, who lived in New Jersey, had purchased his first three-bedroom home. He had not yet taken down the 1950s wallpaper; however, he had taken the time to enlarge and frame three black-and-white photos of my parents and me, which hung on one of the walls. This loving gesture inspired me to take him up on the offer to move in and help with rent.

This was my escape ticket from New York.

With no job, no plan, and a fresh start, I had no clue what to do with my life. I remember being depressed, giving away possessions, and saying cryptic things to my brother that frightened him, no longer finding any reason to live. Out of desperation, I signed up for a course in advertizing design, though found working with Photoshop and Quark Express to be hard on my eyes, frustrating me to tears.

I had befriended a professor of mine who invited me to go dancing on a blind date with her and her boyfriend. One day I remembered telling her that I thought there was something wrong with me, because I could not understand why learning to use graphic design technology was overwhelming me. I attributed some of my struggling to culture shock from moving back to the suburbs from the big city.

One night, while watching the New York Yankees play in the World Series, I fell asleep with my neck crutched in my hand. I woke with a violent migraine. My primary care physician at the time said he saw a red line of tension in my neck and advised me to take three Advil every four hours.

The approaching blind date caused me additional anxiety, though I rationalized that being on a dance floor would help with the mood issues I was experiencing. I attempted to put on my contacts, but both were torn and I had to find an optometrist who would let me walk out with a pair of lenses.

Of all places, the Walmart optometrist, Dr. Bak, in Princeton, New Jersey, could see me. He dilated my pupils and performed two field vision tests. After three hours, he concluded that I had large blind spots in both of my eyes. He said I could have been born with them, but he wanted to investigate further.

I purchased the lenses I needed for the blind date, which by the way was a bore, and scheduled an appointment for a brain scan on the advice of my doctor. My mother came with me to the radiology appointment. This was the first time anyone in my family had been in a Magnetic Resonance Imaging (MRI) tube. The radiologist wouldn't let me leave and called us back to the reading room. He had determined that I had a mass in the bi-occipital region of my brain. I was to wait for the surgeon upstairs. I was freaking out, feeling every emotion possible simultaneously. I went from my knees buckling from underneath me in despair, to laughing thinking that "once they crack your head open you are never the same!"

We met with the surgeon. The films were placed on the light box and when my mother saw the four by five inch brain mass, she fainted.

I recall saying, "I can do all things through Christ who strengthens me." Instantly, I felt zapped with a ray of energy that seemed to resonate from somewhere other than this physical world.

I began to make jokes, asking if this meant that I would have to have my head shaved like GI Jane. The ray of energy filled me with positive light and I knew that I would be fine. All I needed to do was surrender to my higher power.

I was miraculously given the ability to block out negative thoughts and turn inwards to a loving embrace. I had three weeks to ruminate before surgery was performed by renowned cerebrovascular surgeon, Laligam Sekhar (pronounced Shake-her), at George Washington University Hospital in Washington, DC. Dr. Sekhar was a kind Indian man who told me that my tumor was the largest he had ever seen. I asked him if there was anything I could do to make his job easier, and he said, "Pray for the surgeon".

Dr. Sekhar's lead nurse gave me Rosary Beads, which I quickly learned how to use from reading a pamphlet. Surrounding myself with candles and comfortable clothing, I started working with a neuropsychologist who performed a four-hour pre-operative evaluation on me.

I began to use the Rosary daily to self-sooth myself and to meditate in silence. The two-part surgery was comprised of an embolization, performed while awake through the carotid artery in my leg, sending pellets to block blood-flow to kill the tumor. I remember being in such agony for three days, until I gave in to taking pain medication. When the medication began to work, I jumped up and asked to go to the Smithsonian to see the Hope Diamond!

Five days later, the tumor was removed. The nurses in the hospital treated my family and I with great compassion. The surgery left me legally blind and in the intensive care unit (ICU) for several days.

When I awoke from the brain surgery in ICU, I was so happy to be alive I kissed my hands! I was high as a kite on morphine and steroids that I hallucinated for several days. I enjoyed the hallucinations as if it were entertaining artwork.

I was unable to sleep for many days. I arrived home to hundreds of cards, flowers, balloons, and gifts. I remember feeling overwhelmed. I thought my independence had been taken from me. Though I was legally blind for months, I attended neurocognitive therapy for two hours, twice weekly, asking for answers to questions, such as "What is the difference between the mind, brain, and the soul?"

I recall hearing on the radio, "You should pick a goal you cannot reach without God's help." I decided I wanted to go to graduate school and help others find a path of meaning and purpose in this life.

This had occurred around the time of the Columbine shootings. I was inspired to give back to the community. I wanted to understand human suffering and how it can be transformed into healing, health, and wholeness. When I was accepted into the master's program in counselor education at The College of New Jersey, I kissed the ground with gratitude!

Counseling would be the way I could find purpose and existential meaning. Giving back to the community would provide me with a forum where I could talk about spirituality, teach mindfulness meditation, holistic health, and coping skills to others. I struggled with my eyesight and had coordination difficulties.

Through all this, I found that speaking from my soul to guide others to align with their own inherent body-wisdom was my gift from God. As an internal mental coach, I could help others work through difficult life issues. I could show people that life was a gift that offered a level of personal value, which money could not.

Prior to finding my niche in the counseling field, I worked for the radiology company that discovered my brain tumor. As a clinical research project coordinator, I worked with patient data for pharmaceutical oncology trials. After I was weaned off of seizure and thyroid medications I found myself in a rut performing repetitious-monotonous tasks and I experienced terrible insomnia, which put me out of work on disability.

I started to ask myself existential questions, such as, "Can you die from boredom?" I sought out the help of a therapist, who diagnosed me with generalized anxiety disorder, possibly related to organic brain trauma (from having a three-pound mass removed from my cranium).

Realizing my soul was unhappy I decided to volunteer for a local suicide hotline. One night, I received two suicide calls and felt a surge of adrenaline, like a natural high, inspiring me to quit my job and use my counseling degree.

I began a seven-year arduous road to obtain my license in counseling. I met a recovering addict while working in a community agency. Her personal breakthrough inspired me: "It's all green, read it, it's all green God wrote it!"

I had no idea this would become the name of my company. I have worked with hundreds, perhaps thousands of men, women, children, individuals, couples, family systems, and groups in the past twelve years discovering healing, health, and happiness. I am grateful for the calling and the gift to help others discover their own natural strengths, purpose, and meaning in a world filled with so many questions.

The human body is a miraculous entity. It has innate potentiality to manifest health and co-create healing on many levels. I now teach others to *thrive – not just survive!* My journey back to health has been a wake-up call and reminder.

Wellness is a co-creative, ongoing process. It incorporates the mind and body in a spiritual manner to heal the self. And with great hope, our planet, through human connection and soul purpose, will become a place of positive energy and awareness of the power we all have in manifesting great life experiences.

About the Author

Michelle Renee' Bernardo is the Founder and CEO of *It's All Green Wellness, LLC,* located in Princeton Junction, New Jersey, in the United States. She is a national board certified and licensed professional counselor, certified holistic health coach, and marriage and family therapist. Michelle is a member of the National Counseling Association, The American Association of Drugless Practioners, honoree of Sigma Chi Iota National Counseling Honors Society, and Douglas Borough's Professional Commitment Award.

She specializes in mind-body spiritual health using food and lifestyle changes to improve quality of life. Her approach to psychological and physical health is integrative, borrowing techniques from cognitive behavior therapy, mindfulness and Eastern philosophies, reality therapy, holistic health and wellness, family systems theories, existentialism, and spirituality. *It's All Green Counseling Services* offers individual, couples, family therapy, group counseling, and holistic health coaching. Michelle is a certified holistic health counselor and lifelong learner/immersionist of *The Institute for Integrative Nutrition.*

http://www.itsallgreencounselingservices.com

WHEN YOU DON'T KNOW YOU ARE LOVE

Lisa A. Romano

Most of my life, I have felt like a square that believed it was supposed to be a circle. It was normal to feel ill, unsure, confused, and irregular. Feeling as if I did not belong was my everyday state of being. Those I loved did little, if anything, to soothe my chaffed skin or feed my hungry soul. They knew I was bruised from trying to fit in, and did little to ease my experience. This knowing was a conscious one, and it stung my heart like angry wasps.

I wore my sense of irregularity like one would an overcoat. As a young child, I did not know I was so translucent. I presumed the chip on my shoulder was made of armor. I could never have known that the constant bullying I received from my peers at school was being drawn to me like a moth to a flame.

Turns out, my overcoat was made of glass.

When living became too painful, death called out to me like a life preserver thrown into a churning sea. All I wanted to do was to swim and cling to it to finally feel safe. I remember distinctly the splinter of awareness that was born in my reflection that day. There, in front of my parents' bedroom mirror I stood, with a gun pressed firmly against my right temple. The image startled me into the present and shook loose the padlock that had had my chest of grief locked up for so long. Like bats out of Hell, the emotions I had learned to deny sprang forth.

So accustomed to believing my feelings didn't matter, it was surreal to be unable to escape myself emotionally in those moments. There, as streams of pain swam from the corners of my eyes, it was impossible for me not to feel *real*. This sense of visibility was so foreign to my experience, it nearly gobbled me up. Like the crash of thunder after the lightning strikes, a voice entered my awareness and offered me this unsolicited advice: "Lisa, put down the gun. One day you will show them."

In spite of my exasperation over the disconnection I felt from my own family, and the bullying I had been experiencing at school, I put down the gun and miraculously clung to the splinters of consequence which the spirit of awareness had gifted me in those desperate moments. Something bigger than me, and far greater than my perception of my experiences, had been summoned. This *something* I could not name or identify when I was twelve or thirteen, but I knew deep in my soul that whatever this something was, it was real.

And so was I.

Low self-worth plagued me much of my life. It took me more than three decades to gain the objectivity needed to piece together the puzzle that had become my life. As my life progressed, I developed various addictions to help distract me from the disarray my faulty programming and conditioning had created. Food gave me comfort in one moment and swamped me with guilt in the next, while exercise compulsion did its best to play the middle-man. Feeling powerless most of my life, compounded by the belief that my feelings were worthless, my mind gravitated towards food not only in search of a commiserating friend, but for a sense of control as well.

By the time I was in my mid-thirties, my body had become riddled with inflammatory diseases like asthma, migraines, and unexplainable rashes. When my allergist told me I needed to start listening to my body because my body was listening to me, once again my pinhole-sized concept of the awareness I had of my *self* expanded.

Additionally, I was suffering from a severe panic disorder. My panic attacks had gotten so bad by my mid-thirties, that often I felt as if I were melting away under a thick layer of tar. As if my body was quite literally being drained of its life force, panic was robbing me of my life. I entered therapy to help me gain some control over what was happening in my mind. During that time, despite being too distracted by the physical manifestations going on in my body as the result of my negative belief systems, I did latch onto the idea that my subconscious thought processes had something to do with the fact that both my parents were adult children of alcoholics.

By the age of thirty-three I had seen enough of the discontented life I had created. So ingrained within my subconscious the notion that I was not enough, I had drawn into my experience the very things I consciously believed I did not want. So comfortable with thinking love was something I needed to earn, I manifested a life that did little more than create a loop of yearning rather than receiving. Love, acceptance, forgiveness, understanding, validation, empathy, and compassion were not amongst my vibrational offerings, although I believed they were. Instead, I offered to the world all that I believed on a subconscious level what I was; I simply was not enough.

I had not been taught to love my *self*. I had not been taught to care more about what I thought about myself than what others thought about me. I had not been taught that I was worthy, simply because I existed. Instead I was programmed to look outside of myself for acceptance, and as a result I attracted those who were more than eager to keep me chasing after that acceptance. My life, and all the things I said I detested about it, was a manifestation of who I emotionally was on a vibrational level.

My marriage ended shortly after I turned thirty-three, although in my soul I know it ended long before that. A therapist who specialized in co-dependent recovery guided me toward paths that he knew I needed to explore. With vigor and zeal, I pulled myself up from the abyss that followed my divorce, turned from almost all those I believed loved me, and set out in search of my healing.

In the twelve years that have passed since my divorce, my life has been nothing but waves of miracles one after the next. As I learned to detach myself from those who stirred negative emotions within me, my thoughts became lighter and my vibrational offerings began to change. My heart became highly saturated with a desire for peace and, as a result of the contrast the first part of my life had created, my mind focused with intent only upon those things that were able to bring me joy.

In the early days when money was still scarce, and when I was struggling to help my three small children make sense of the mess that had become their life, I forced myself to be grateful for things that would otherwise make life such a misery to live in, like the fact that I had clear drinking water coming through my faucets, or that I could walk, talk, and breath. All the things that I had once taken so blindly for granted, I began to fall in love with. And as I did, the Universe rewarded my gratefulness with circumstances, people, and ideas that brought about more peace.

If I have learned anything in this lifetime it is this: All that is exists because of the life force energy. And all that is, is a manifestation of that life force energy regardless of what it manifests itself in the form of; a human being, a butterfly, or a drop of rain. There is no such thing as separateness. On the quantum level, we are all entangled, drawing to ourselves not what we think we want, but what we are. The Universe does not judge. It makes no difference to the Universe whether you believe you were destined to be poor or otherwise. The Universe does not think. It is but a vibrational dimension whether we believe it or not, and works more simply than we have been conditioned and programmed to realize.

I have also learned that all love starts with self-love. It is not possible to love others, when your subconscious mind does not accept and believe that you are worthy of love, nor is it possible to find the love you consciously tell yourself you are in search of. When your vibrational offering is one of lack, only more lack can manifest, which is why the love of self truly is the cornerstone of all joyous life experiences.

It is possible to heal from within. I know this because my life is proof of so. My healing did not show up overnight, nor did my diseases. Once I understood that *I* was not bad, or, better said, once I realized that the same life Source that created the Universe created me, and that it was my thinking that was bad, I began to think more deliberately on a conscious level. As my focus to more pleasant ideas increased, so did my level of joy. And as my life began to feel more effortless I more consciously appreciated the power of my own mind. A lack of deliberate focus, fueled by my conditioning to react rather than think, infused my being with layers of sadness and quite literally manifested as anxiety and disease in my body.

These days I am happy to be a square. I no longer swim upstream or try to beat to the drum of others. I accept others for who they are even if *who they are* doesn't like me very much. I understand that bad things happen for the sake of contrast. Without it, none of us would know when we were headed in the wrong direction. I know now I was not supposed to die that day in the mirror. The Universe knew how deeply my desire to feel connected to others was. It is my prayer that through the sharing of some of my life's story, that you in some way feel more connected to you, to the earth, to the sky, and perhaps even to me.

You are loved. You are enough. Grief showed up, when you temporarily forgot these truths and disconnected from Source. The magnificent thing about being a conscious creator, however, is that once you *get it* and awaken, you begin to understand that joy is but a deliberate focused thought away. The more deliberate your focus, the more deliberate a creator you become in the reality of this space-time continuum, and the more effortless your ability becomes to manifest the life you desire.

Namaste.

About the Author

Lisa A. Romano was born and raised in Queens, New York. She is a writer and self-help specialist. As a life coach, Lisa has transformed the lives of hundreds of her clients through key understandings such as self-awareness and self-responsibility. Lisa specializes in the areas of low self-esteem, co-dependency, enabling, and self-love.

Lisa's personal struggles and ultimate triumphs over co-dependency, low self-worth, and various addictions have laid the backdrop for a life dedicated to helping others heal their faulty childhood programming, so that they may learn to deliberately manifest the life they desire now. Her deep understanding of the mind, body, and the soul, and the connection to the Universe itself, is easy to understand, riveting, healing, and mind-expanding.

Her work is all about healing; much needed by the world's people today. Lisa touches souls and heals hearts through her writing.

http://www.healingselfesteem.com/

DECODING THE MIND OF GOD

O.M. Kelly

I grew up in the Australian outback, miles from our next-door neighbor, where nature was my childhood friend. My father told me stories of Einstein's Theory of Relativity in a child-like way, and challenged me to explore more when I had time on my hands. My life matured into adulthood. I fell in love, married, and raised a large family on a cattle-raising property.

In the 80s, we sold our property and turned to restaurants, thinking life would be easier. Working nearly 24/7 to keep the customer satisfied, I eventually became ill and collapsed, and was admitted to the hospital.

There, I gently slipped into a coma.

I still recall what had happened during this fascinating experience, as I was free to travel the planet. I awoke to be told I had diabetes from a sheer overload of stress. My doctor asked me to sell up and slow down and asked me if I had ever tried meditation. I had not, and so he gave me a phone number of a local woman who was a meditation teacher to ring.

Finally finding the courage, I did so and the rest was history.

I began to see a new pathway manifesting as my interest grew through discovering this ancient art of meditation, and realized that the information I was receiving from my teacher was inviting me into unknown territory.

The new words I heard her speak were not in my dictionary of common sense. I listened to her stories of other worlds and felt myself transforming into a child once again and realized that I had began a new education in a new school. I felt that I had left my old home town and was living in a new suburb in my mind.

Over time, my body grew from strength to strength; this new thinking came to monopolize my whole perspective on what my life was truly all about! My thirst for this ancient knowledge began to consume me the deeper I stepped into this inner world.

What had I accomplished to earn this next encounter? Was I really this important?

Teachers entered my life and everything took on a new meaning, as I began to understand that everything had a mathematical form.

"There are no mistakes. These are the natural universal laws that surround our planet, where everything adds up all by itself, as you will too, the more you get to know yourself. What you need to know, ask the question. Then reverse your question back to *yourself* and you will find the answer," I was told.

Years of training began and for the first time in my life I found comfort in *me*, and I became my own best friend!

In time I was asked to read the Bible backwards and my excitement grew as I began to understand these hidden codes that others talked about. I was finally beginning to understand how the authors had written their books to help us understand our reason for being here.

As a child it had been explained to me that the Bible was written to explain our **Basic Information Before Leaving Earth**. Wow! This sounded like Star Wars stuff and the words stuck with me over the years, until I had finished my journey to know exactly what these ancient authors were explaining.

I understood that the written word so often mentioned in the Bible is our recorded memories of everything that has ever been, is and will be, and that it has been embedded in every cell of our body since the beginning of time.

Remember: We are made in the likeness of God! It is written *within* us.

This is the scribe we see through the hieroglyphs of the Egyptian philosophies. Through reading the Bible backwards I began to understand a different version to what I had been taught as a child.

I spoke to my father – who was my first teacher – and explained my journey to him; he mentioned the words *metaphor, metaphorical,* and *metaphysics*, and the more I understood my teachings the more I realized I was metabolically retracing my own *matter of physics*. I was nourishing myself through my own thinking. My genes could unfurl their information the more I could induce myself. So, this was how the ancient mathematics still continued to work through the original plan from the time of the big bang.

The more I began to understand the true meanings of ancient myths, especially those belonging to the Akkadian, Egyptian, Grecian, Indian, Tibetan, Asian, and Mayan philosophies, and the reasoning behind the codes to 2012, the more I understood this ancient language.

No: The world is not going to end!

These codes have a totally different interpretation. I soon realized I had a story to tell so that we could understand this ancient language and get the story right, as it is only through an open heart that all wars are won!

My mind opened up to the sacred codes of numerology, which were threaded throughout the pages of the Bible. I finally came to understand why Adam was a hundred and thirty years old before he sired his son, and how he continued to live another eight hundred years. Nine hundred and thirty years he spent on Earth before he died! Now that is a good inning.

And what about Noah?

He was six hundred before he had to go out and build the ark. Then he lived until he was nine hundred and fifty years old. Wow! What a quest he had undertaken. I was elated to know that I had finally cracked the codes to the Bible!

As one teacher finished, another one took their place and initiated me into my next step. Each time I peeled off another layer to these inner secrets, I could understand another depth of how we allow ourselves through our innocence to add to the creation of the original psychoses of the mind. As soon as the information was understood, I had to climb another rung of the ladder of my own DNA.

"Move on!" My teachers explained. "You're not there yet!"

I began to understand the importance of our thinking: what a thought is, where it comes from, what we do with it, and where it goes. I found that it depended on how we brought forth our thoughts as to how our inner mathematics autonomically created a sentence for us to speak!

The learning's introduced me into how our inner mathematics is permanently connected to our thoughts, where they are free to create a life force of their own. I found that each disease we attract to ourselves also used the same mathematics to create itself in its own time. It simply depended on how long we hung on to a past experience we had already lived, and how our ego had been ostracized through an excuse it had created for its self at that time.

My God! We are our own worst enemy!

Again the mathematics stepped forward to present me with the information as to why we die. It all depended on how our intellect echoed throughout our tribe as to how it was delivered to the cosmos.

There is this grand plan that we don't want to know about; it is all around us and is working for us every moment of our lives. And my lessons continued right up to understanding the knowledge of the sacred alphabet regarding the Egyptian philosophies to extraterrestrial intelligence, and how this sentence of us earning our *basic information before leaving Earth* collected itself.

This went on for years, as I shredded my fingernails to the bone and bloodied my knees and toes, climbing the rockiest and sheerest of cliff faces one could possibly imagine; all to recall this information and bring it to our attention.

It was explained to me that this is where our knowledge becomes wisdom. In other words, it becomes easier when we have an idea of how the truth of all things is explaining to us where we are heading.

Finally I was told that I had earned my totem and had completed the education of becoming a fully fledged Shaman and Avatar, where I helped create the elements of air, fire, earth, and water, and that the world awaited my teachings!

Instantly the promoters stepped in asking me to join them and over the next three years, I lectured seven days a week to thousands of people around Australia. I then stepped out of my own boundaries after an invitation came from New Zealand. Other lands soon followed and invited me. I accepted the invitations and found that with each new land I walked into, I would be met by the elder and be initiated into becoming a tribal elder of their spoken language. It was an honor to wear the garments that they presented to me, while I was a guest in their land.

Regardless of what language we speak, we all have the same identical mannerisms to overcome. I found people coming out of their forests from all walks of life; from the Jackaroo in the outback to the university professor, they all heard my words.

"Where's your book?" came their call.

"I haven't had time to write it yet," I answered.

I received invitations from other countries on the other side of the planet and in the mid-nineties I accepted an invitation to lecture in Germany. The crowds built up and I was asked to stay and teach. Before long, other invitations came from other countries where I was soon explaining my teachings in eight languages a week! All is fully explained in my book *Decoding the Mind of God*. The information continues to bring the never-ending story together in the following book *Decoding the Book of Revelations*.

Over the years, the students gathered and I kept on needing larger premises to house them. A castle was offered to me and we all worked together and renovated it back into its former glory. The temple was ready and for the next seven years the teachings were in earnest. Those students who came from other lands could also earn themselves. The interpreters grew and as the seminars commenced, I felt like we were our own United Nations.

The students came and each time I spoke, my cup would refill with new information. The more I believed in me, the more I unfurled the codes that were secreted throughout my DNA. The information kept on advancing each time I stepped deeper into these ancient codes to reveal our next educated step.

Knowledge has never ceased. It is right at our fingertips. We do not have to stretch far to reach for it.

My secretaries typed my words into English and sent them back to Australia where they were placed into hundreds of pigeon holes to create the foundation of my future books. Over the years my days grew into nights as we collected around 9,000 pages of information and the next step presented itself into me becoming an author.

My passion became my purpose to return to Australia to dedicate myself to writing my earnings, and to bring this amazing story together where all of the ancient wisdom is brought into the moment, through announcing to us our next thought. As I wrote one story, another one followed and the information kept revealing itself to explain how important you are.

Your success is through your spirituality healing you from within.

I realized I could now begin to tell you the story as to how the sciences of Egyptology, the Holy Bible, the principles of the Mayan, Grecian, and the Indo-Asian mythology, and finally the medical agenda are all explaining the exact same story. Only the names have been changed to protect the innocent.

Yes, everything is as it should be! The Universe awaits your proprietary earnings to explain to you that we are all made in the likeness of God.

About the Author

O.M. Kelly, known as Omni, is an accomplished author and lecturer on metaphysics, philosophy, and the natural order of consciousness. Her works explain how we all evolve into the unconscious mind. The years of personal research has led to discoveries and initiations into the universal mathematical language; all compiled into a nine volume tutorial masterpiece.

Omni was asked to read the Bible backwards from Revelations to Genesis. She came to realize that she was reading the same stories as the hieroglyphs were explaining in Egypt. Her mind took on a greater challenge to recall this ancient information and bring the story together, all of which coincides with the pyramids and temples. Omni established a teaching academy in Germany, initiating others into her teachings where, to their surprise, they discovered the importance of these laws was also embedded in their genes.

Open any page to discover more about your own truth.

http://www.elanea.com

THE MAGIC OF CONSCIOUSNESS

Petra Stampfer

I immigrated to Australia from Germany in 2007, arriving after twenty-seven years of service for a well-established travel company, experiencing an interesting and diverse, but a stressful, career. By the time I reached Melbourne, I was ready to change my life.

I'd studied life coaching, kinesiology, crystal massage, and, looking for relief from ongoing headaches, I'd started practicing meditation. Four months into my new life in Melbourne, I spotted an ad in a holistic magazine for enrolments in a diploma in meditation teaching. It called me.

Partway through the course, all twenty students had to attend a week-long retreat entitled *The Journey of Enlightenment and Wellbeing*. To participate, we were told we'd have to let go of all distractions: reading, mobile phones, music, and even watches and jewelry.

Already this was wildly new to me.

Next came some of my internal hopes and questions: "Will this week change my view that life is a struggle, even though I experience lots of happy days? Will I experience more inner light?" And the big one: "What does enlightenment mean?"

My intentions for the retreat were set: to feel lighter, happier, healthier, and to lose weight, given that that yummy vegetarian food would be our diet! Yet I had mixed feelings as day one approached. *What would my personal journey be like? Would I understand everything?*

"Well, for a start you are very brave, Petra." I tried to encourage myself.

After a short introduction on the first day we were forbidden to speak with each other, except during official sessions as a group and with our two facilitators. This was out of everyone's comfort zones, including mine. Between sessions we had to contemplate and journal whatever arose from group sessions and exercises. Opening and sharing myself in the group sessions became easier with each passing day and I slowly gained more trust in the process. After all, I reminded myself, "I'm here to take the next step in my life, to become a meditation teacher and to clear my mental and emotional clutter."

The group sessions covered various modalities, from transpersonal psychology, shamanism, dance therapy, and self-hypnosis to ego-state therapy and active communication skills. In these sessions I sensed a united aim: to improve the connection with my *higher self*; that part that is infinitely wise that allows me to express my true self.

"Tell me who you are?" was the question I was confronted with daily. "Who am I really, behind the everyday mask?" The deeper I dug, the more the old stuff surfaced. How could I free myself from that? How could I let go of what no longer served me? How could I become more compassionate, loving, creative, vibrant? It felt like I was walking a labyrinth in my mind. Fighting demons and the search for my essence, my soul search had begun.

Day by day my self-image and self-confidence changed. My intuition and self-worth emerged and I started seeing where I was sabotaging myself. I was tapping beyond body, thoughts, and feelings beyond what I could consciously know about myself. I realized that if I could let go of dysfunctional habits, guilt, blame, and regrets, rewards like self-love, joy, and fun were within reach.

And then came *rebirthing*: a powerful daily session of a practice that was completely new to me. Rebirthing is a breathing technique that allows the breather to directly tap into their consciousness and let go of previously suppressed material. It works on all levels: body, mind, emotions, and spirit.

Each session ran for up to two hours and, under the guidance of a rebirthing professional, involved lying on a mattress and relaxing with music while focusing on continual connected breathing. There were no pauses between inhalations and exhalations. Entering this state, we were told, would energize the body and could bring up old memories, feelings, and tensions.

During the first four sessions, I felt distracted and overwhelmed by the group energy. "That distraction has to stop!" I urged myself. But for this to work, I needed clarity and a clear intention. *How else could I work towards releasing whatever was preventing me from living life to its fullest?*

Rebirthing

Breathing in and out, connecting the inhales with the exhales, and feeling my body, connecting with my feelings, I am letting go of all negative thoughts and tensions. I keep breathing that connected breath, but my mouth is getting dry. I fall into a meditative state.

Feelings of "I don't want to be on Earth" arise. A picture of God and myself appears, both pulling at a rope. I see and feel that I am tearing on one end of the rope and God is pulling on the other. My body begins to cramp and I try to relax and surrender, but there is so much fear around living this life. I visualize myself in earlier spiritual lives, experiencing lots of violence and pain. My body feels so heavy and tense, yet I continue breathing. Shivers roll down my spine and several parts of my body start tingling, like old hurtful information wants to be erased, out of my tissue, out of my cells. Strong pain spikes one side of my face, centering on my jaw, but I bravely breathe through it.

The body holds its own wisdom and memory. It wants to heal.

My mind kicks in and wants me to know this pain must originate from the forceps the doctors used on me when I was born to speed up a stagnated delivery. I continue breathing in and out, letting go of tension, becoming more aware of the music in the room, and relaxing more and more. Though I sense numbness in my body, I make it to the end of the session feeling at peace.

Going into the next session, countless thoughts wander through my mind. I'm nervous but I'm not sure why. Calling on spiritual guidance seems the best I can do to help get me through. Eventually, the connected breathing and relaxing the tension from my body helps calm my mind.

I feel safe.

After breathing for some time, emotions start to surface. I'm holding the intent to go right back to the traumatic emotion of my birth. Fear arises. My mother and I are connected in that fear. I tell her, "I

146

love you, Mom," in search of love myself. But there *is* no love! Feeling discouraged, a deep sadness arises. I make God responsible. God brought me into this situation, to live this life here on Earth. I'm struggling with Him on this matter.

I start coughing and throwing up slime. Then I sense two people looking after me. I feel safe again. A voice, close to my right ear, says, "Keep breathing!" And I do; in and out with an emerging awareness and understanding that it was my choice, that I had wanted this earthly experience, and that I had chosen my parents. A vision of them emerges before my inner eyes. They look very young, the way they must have looked before conceiving me. My breathing is calming though I'm still focused on my intent. I want to give everything I can to release that old stuff from my consciousness and clear my channel to God. The breath-flow continues, in and out, focusing on that connected breath.

My lower back starts hurting and I'm moving my pelvis up and down then bringing my knees to my chest. My head hurts incredibly. I can sense the energy is stuck in there and I can feel the pressure of the forceps on my temples.

I start crying, not standing the pain. I'm coughing, throwing up slime over and over again. My throat is in agony. "Please God, help me out of this situation!"

Then, "My angels, please help me get through this!"

I sense an earth angel next to my head. She is supporting me with her healing hands, helping me release the blockage there. It's so congested. There is still so much pain in my lower back and now it is spreading to my belly. I curl my legs so that my knees are near my chest again and entwine my arms around them. There is full pressure on my belly now. The position releases some of the pain but I'm still throwing up. Suddenly the pressure re-intensifies.

"Surrender!" says a voice close to my right ear. I'm lying on that mattress, torn between Heaven and Hell, between birth and death, between this dimension and others.

Breakthrough

"Yes, I want to set myself free!" I scream. I'm screaming the hell out of me. I have the feeling that my head could explode anytime. A facilitator puts strong pressure on my bent knees, thereby on my belly. It feels like I'm simultaneously rebirthing and giving birth, somewhere between Heaven and Earth.

I hear the same whisper close to my right ear. "Surrender!"

"Oh, my God, all angelic beings, please help me! I can't take that pressure and pain any longer!" I pray silently while screaming the place down. "Oh, my God! Yes, yes, yes, I will surrender! Yes, I give up all resistance and resentment. I surrender to all these long-buried feelings and let them go. Please, save me God!"

While I experience peak pain and pressure, in the next moment there is a shift. I find myself in a different space. I see my body from the outside, watching it from above. It's a magical feeling, as if all struggle, pain, resistance, and burden have been released through that shift in consciousness.

There is only bliss. There is only light; white-golden light. I'm travelling through different dimensions of the light. I'm connected to Source energy. This is where I belong. I am a being of the light, a child of the Universe, feeling the love and joy, beyond words. I am connected to all that is and all that will ever be. God is everything. I am a part of God. I am one with God. I am that I am. God wants nothing. There is love everywhere. I start laughing.

All pain and struggle is forgotten.

"I love you all so much!" A shout of joy ends the session and I'm laughing from the deepest reaches of my heart and soul. Everyone in the room starts laughing too. It is done.

Healing from within

My intuition told me to surrender everything to God. On the other side of fear, pain, hurt, anger, resentment, antagonism, hostility, grief, uncertainty, confusion, guilt, and separation are love, peace, acceptance, and oneness.

And while this bliss hasn't stayed with me ever since (a reminder that I'm not totally enlightened!), I've learned every bliss by a big shift in consciousness, like an onion where you peel off layer by layer. And there are many layers to the core.

Since then I have a different view on life. I'm more aware of what is happening around me; of the bigger picture. My ability to relax into this precious existence has increased tremendously, so has my trust. Trusting the light, my feelings, thoughts, intuition, and instincts opened me to a deeper understanding of life, love, and higher wisdom. Knowing that spirit is working in and through each of us gives me a deep sense of relaxation and ease. I follow my heart though I often need to free myself from my busy mind.

To experience *inner freedom*, I meditate daily, enjoy energy-work and crystal-therapy, and control my attitude. I keep spiritual values high and follow my guidance. Most importantly, I've gained faith in myself, in others, and in the Universe.

Every ounce of my commitment and surrender was worth it; to get to the other side no matter what! There on that mattress, screaming until I found surrender, I found the greatest love of all inside of me.

About the Author

Raised in Bavaria, Germany, Petra now lives in Melbourne, Australia, where she founded the Soul Light Institute of Massage and Holistic Healing in 2008, offering treatments, trainings, and workshops in complementary therapies.

Petra's spiritual journey started at the age of forty. The name Petra comes from the Greek word *petros*, meaning stone or rock. No wonder gemstones and crystals captivated her when she first encountered them at age thirty. Today she applies them to her work in crystal light healing and energy healing, crystal massage and reflexology, and chakra balancing.

An intuitive life and spiritual coach, Petra also uses dowsing rods for healing work and draws on her broad knowledge of symbols and the body's energy pathways for healing with humans and animals.

Petra's commitment to helping people bring their health and life in balance forms part of her vision for peace, harmony, and freedom in the world.

http://www.petrastampfer.com

I AM MY HEALING

Gerardine Hillier

Everyone wants to heal. It is the reason we read self-help books, attend personal development workshops, or try therapy. It is why we bury ourselves in our busy life, avoiding, if possible, our grief and pain. The tendency is to see healing as *getting better* and therefore another goal for which to strive.

This in fact *may* take us away from actually healing.

To heal means to restore to wholeness; to reconcile. To reconcile means to be no longer opposed. So what in us is in opposition? Well, there is only one answer. We are in opposition to our self. It is not about striving to attain something but to rediscover what has always been there: our wholeness.

We begin life with this wholeness. It is there in the eyes of each new-born. It is a wisdom and a mystery. Our awareness of this wholeness gradually becomes fractured by the input we receive on our journey through life as we are constantly being told who we are. We are fed conflicting ideas of right and wrong, good and bad, acceptance and rejection. This acquired knowledge in turn creates our beliefs and our patterns of behavior. It becomes the filter through which we perceive ourselves, our experiences, and the world. It becomes our way of being, and it draws to itself more of the same.

My own journey began as a simple, ordinary life. I was part of a large family. A humble, suburban home and yard was my domain, and I spent my early years feeling safe; lost in a fantasy of dreams and play. Because I was part of a large family, I managed to escape constant attention. My hours of being alone were sacred because, during these times, I still felt my wholeness. I have very early recollections of this *knowing of self*.

A series of events shattered my peaceful world. When I was nine, we moved from my childhood home to a new house in a fledgling neighborhood of new houses. Eighteen months later my mother died. She was forty-seven. I adored my mother, especially the feel of her love and nurture and the warmth of her smile. I was in no way ready to be without her.

What ensued was a troubled adolescence. I ran away from a home that no longer felt like a sanctuary, trying to find *myself* in a generation of protest, free love, drugs, and a desire to change the world. Inevitably I was incarcerated in a detention center for uncontrollable adolescents. No one ever talked about disenfranchised grief and my unexpressed pain continued to create patterns of fear and rejection. It was a time of loss and lonely wandering.

My father died when I was seventeen. His last years had become a muddled haze of alcohol and broken dreams. I drifted away from my familial ties, and in due course I became a wife and mother. I discovered my safety nets, mainly writing and yoga, which offered me support and fed my spirit. But the undercurrent of my life was still fear, doubt, and a deep aching loneliness. I loved my husband, children, and rural home surrounded by nature, but I could not heal the ache that often robbed the vibrancy from my life.

The opportunity to express and heal came through yet another loss: the death of a soul mate and mentor. It was as if, once again, the one who most supported and reflected my wholeness was taken away. The difference this time was that I did not deny myself the experience of pain and grief. I walked that journey step by step. I immersed myself in it, went right to its core, and, in doing so, felt the joy that comes with true understanding.

When I thought I was finished with the grief and loss, I had a disturbing dream. In it was a young woman with an unsightly, prominent scar down her face. I stood before this woman and, touching her face with great tenderness, I said, "You must heal this scar."

When I awoke in the morning, I knew the scar was mine but I did not understand the message. I had fully experienced my grief and loss, not only the recent one but the frayed threads of all the grief from my past. I knew I had done so because the change in my life was profound. I had once again found my inner voice and I was learning to trust it.

Opportunities for growth rapidly presented themselves. I understood what it meant to stand alone and to become self reliant. I discovered that death is powerless to end a life; nothing is ever taken away from us. What healing was still to be done?

That afternoon, as was my usual custom, I walked up a hill on my property to a place where I used to sit in daily meditation. All the way, an incessant voice was urging me to heal my scar.

I did not know what I was meant to do.

Suddenly I became aware that a most magnificent sunset was taking place all around me and I had been so lost in my thoughts I had not noticed. The sky was awash with breathtaking colors as layers of soft cloud were illuminated by orange, red, and gold. It seemed as if the whole world had stopped to watch such splendor unfolding, and even the birds were silent. There was also a need in me to stay still and witness this miracle of color, light, and patterns.

"What is it you ask of me?" I asked Creation.

The answer was like a voice that appeared out of nowhere. "Give it all back. You have a choice. You can hold it and you can claim it as part of *you* or you can offer it back."

Until that point, it had always been my belief that our deep emotional scars stay within us because this had been the knowledge fed to me along with the usual platitudes: *You never really get over it, the sorrow diminishes but it is always with you, there is always an ache,* and so on.

Yet now, I was being given a choice. There was a sudden clutch of fear, for I didn't know how I could give up something that was part of me. What I was really saying was: How can I give up something that I had begun to identify as who I am?

The truth, when it arises, carries a force that brings the *self* to its knees in love and gratitude. I am not my pain and grief. I am not even my joy and bliss. I am not my body, my thoughts, and my experiences.

My life since that time has been an adventure of synchronicity and miracles. It has become a dance that has led me through a whirlwind of experiences, becoming an author, travelling to different countries, creating a center for others to discover their health, peace, hope, and joy, and facilitating classes, workshops, and retreats in yoga, creative expression, and self awareness.

It is a life I once would not have conceived.

I cannot say that there have not been challenges along the way. Life does not come with guarantees. We all die. Dying is interwoven into the fabric of our living. But the wonderful aspect of this life is that any pain and suffering also offers an opportunity for deeper insight; a greater awareness and capacity for understanding and compassion.

We have the power to transcend our pain.

Acceptance is the first step to healing and transcending. Rather than filtering our experiences through the judgmental eyes of our personality, we have the capability to redefine them through the eyes of our knowing, watchful self. Rather than resignation, acceptance asks us to be fully aware of what *is*. Once we fully experience something, we actually stop holding onto it, trying to change it, or manipulate it. In this open awareness, we create the space for change to occur. Any feeling, mood, or experience can be redefined simply by our willingness to shift our perception. If we remain open to what is, in time we learn to accept joy and sorrow for what they are without distinction.

Without this acceptance there is resistance. Through resistance we become closed and brittle, and essentially become trapped in our own suffering.

Life shows me over and over again not to struggle but to simply experience. Not to hold on but to release. Not to fear and doubt but to trust. It has taught me that healing means knowing that the false perception of self is what separates me from my true nature. It is this very separation that creates all suffering. It has taught me that, in essence, I own nothing, have nothing, and that everything belongs to God. This powerful truth offers liberation.

It offers immense freedom.

It is not about my past or future. I have no power in either. It is only in this moment that I have the power to change. Healing happens... now! Not by dragging the past along with me hoping to heal it. Not by clinging to the hope that in the future it shall all be better. It is the healing I can bring to each moment, not just for myself, but for others. Healing comes when we are truly present. Every moment is an opportunity to recognize, accept, acknowledge, and release. It is a treasure of awareness. It sings its newness, its potential, and its vivid aliveness.

In every moment we have the opportunity to be the *beloved*. Every moment spent in Divine awareness, which is in essence awareness of our true nature, is the only time we are truly conscious. This is where healing occurs. Knowing that in each moment we are new, vividly alive, and bursting with enormous potential, brings us back to our wholeness. When I hold Divine awareness, I cannot hold discomfort, be it from fear, sadness, pain, or grief. Where I am encapsulated in calmness and stillness, I am in love.

To heal is to reconcile with our true, constant, unmoving self.

I gave back my journey through grief and loss. All of it. I offered it like a prayer that spread into the ether and, like the sinking sun, disappeared. Only the quiet stillness remained.

The All Knowing Self

There is
a sudden realization;
I always knew you –
always – my forever;
in the flesh of my childhood,
before a knowledge of life
corrupted
the quintessential living of it;
then,
without even knowing
my own breath,
I knew you.

I always loved you –
the mystery of you
that needed no solution;
when I did not feel
to offer my living
as my prayer –

my devotion;
when nothing required
consecration or remembrance
because you
were already here
in my silence.

About the Author

Gerardine (Gerry) Hillier refers to herself as an *ordinary person*. Gerry is a yoga teacher and has taught relaxation and meditation for twenty-six years. For the past ten years, Gerry has been the proprietor and coordinator of a yoga and relaxation center in Queensland, Australia, where she conducts classes, counselling and healing sessions, workshops, and training.

Gerry is also a drama teacher, writer, stage director, and published author who combines her understanding of creative expression with the philosophy of yogic tradition to facilitate self inquiry and healing. Gerry is also a director of The Owl Company in Singapore, promoting creativity and self-awareness.

She lives on a property in the beautiful Noosa Hinterland, Australia. It is her sanctuary and a place of peace and tranquility.

http://www.yogahouse.com.au

THE ALCHEMY OF GRIEF

Annette Chennell

If anything in life is certain, it's death.

Despite this certainty, we often flounder when death comes to carry off someone we love. In the space of only a few years, my sister committed suicide, my mother died, my husband suffered a sudden fatal aneurysm, and my father died after a long period of palliative care. Two close friends of mine also died dramatically; their hearts gave out. Mine followed.

I couldn't have imagined grief of this magnitude.

People gathered as people do, in a ragged ululation. Some strengthened my faith in human kind and friendship. They helped me keep breathing. Sadly, other times the same things were said and done over and over leaving me feeling isolated and misunderstood: a social oddity. Some mumbled, "I'm here for you," as they high-tailed it to the other side of the street, dodging speeding traffic with agility never seen before. Conversations became surreal. "You'll find someone else," was murmured to me at the wake of my husband's death. I wondered if I was hallucinating.

At first I was enraged, but as peace eventually replaced the tears, I saw that just as I was unique in my grief, so were those around me. We are all human. And to lose someone we love is about as human as it gets.

It has been an alchemist's work to distill the things that helped during those nightmarish foggy periods, and those that didn't. This chapter is a chance to demystify the shrouded world of the recently bereaved. It's written for those riding their own midnight grief train to show that you're not alone.

This is what I have learned.

Helplessness

During our grief, people naturally fly to our side. That old rescuer, who has slept dormant inside his rusty armor, wakes up ready to get in there and fix things. Suddenly the house is inundated with visitors, the phone seems possessed. What is clear though is that no one can fix this, no matter how they try. It is beyond anyone to make everything alright. Death is unequivocal and we are reduced in the face of it.

I was swamped by the question: "Is there anything I can do?"

"I don't know," I answered, sure that I looked like an idiot. It was hard to give direction when even getting myself a glass of water seemed like an Olympic challenge. What I really wanted to say was, "Can you make it like it was last week?"

Nothing else would help.

"Call me if you need anything," people would say. But I didn't. I didn't call anyone. I was reluctant to impose or expose need and suffering.

I had to learn gracious acceptance. When I did, it honored my friends, my family, and me; a win-win situation that strengthened bonds forever. Accepting help in that first phase smoothens the passage through the absurd number of things that need to be organized. If there is a friend or family member who is a frustrated sergeant major, bring them on.

"Know that we are all bereft. Be open to the help of others."

Isolation

Death leaves an emptiness that is as jagged as it is new. The absence of what had gone scared the Hell out of me. The emptiness felt like a gaping hole in the center of my chest. But the traffic outside snarled as it always did - school bells ringing amidst the sound of laughing children, and people shopping. It seemed obscene that the sun went up and down with blatant disregard. I lived in another Universe and wondered if or how I would find my way back.

The sense of isolation was reinforced by well meaning friends. "I know how you feel," they said. "I know you must be angry!"

A neighbor, regarding the sudden death of my husband, said, "You must have a little chink in your heart."

No, I feel sick. I have a chasm in my chest.

It is important to look for the sympathy intended, however clumsily. Brave friends admitted they couldn't understand what I was going through. Only then could I admit that I didn't understand either.

The phones and the doorbell did stop ringing. For others, work and everyday concerns soon recaptured their attention. Screaming silence replaced the chaos of the first weeks. One world moved on, while mine didn't.

"You will come to see life as normal again. It takes time, one step at a time. Be patient."

Anger and Forgiveness

Acquaintances and even good friends vanished in my acute phase of grief. Some described how they tried to call but hung up before they dialed. Others explained how they sat in their cars outside my house unable to come in. They didn't know what to say or do. During chance encounters on the street, the death often went unmentioned; they spoke instead of the curtains they'd recently installed.

I wondered if we'd all gone mad.

Over time I forgave all of those seemingly unthinking acts. They did their best, as I did. I forgave myself for my struggle and sensitivity. I forgave the one who'd died, for dying and for all the minor, sometimes major, upsets we'd shared.

Anger arises from, and brings only, pain. Forgiveness arises from, and brings only, love. It was an easy choice.

"Forgiveness is the spiritual cure for anger."

Honoring the Pain

Grief yanks us out of our comfort zone, and someone in pain comes across as a scary unpredictable creature. For me, owning and expressing the pain was a natural and essential part of the healing process. This isn't so for everyone. As I sobbed at the wake of my mother's death, a dear friend told me I was getting too emotional. What she might have meant was that I was getting too emotional for her. I was comfortable in my own discomfort. The pain was excruciating but very real.

Letting the emotional dam burst is necessary. I thought of my *howling to the moon* episodes like contractions during labor. Each one, once over, was another one down. One I'd never have to do again. One step closer to a new state.

The essence of *if only* also brings pain. People feel guilt for many reasons: being the one who survived; not being able to stop death (*if only* we could be super heroes); the argument they had the day before the death.

As time passed, guilt rode on the tail of my first laugh; appreciating a sunny day; being determined to live my life well despite my loss.

"Emotional collapses represent movement. Sit quietly with them. Like a contraction they are easier if you don't fight them. Dispense with guilt. It doesn't help anyone."

We are Unique in Our Grief and Recovery

Grief has its own agenda. There are no rules or timetables (OK, it's Tuesday: time for stage two). Some people around me wanted life to normalize quickly while I chose to trust my own judgment and sit awhile with the abnormality and pain.

One piece of wisdom helped me realize I wasn't mad despite this: that we each have a unique way of experiencing grief and each and every loss is different. If that means sitting on the floor in a heap, go right ahead. If it means scrubbing the bathroom every day, there is no harm in that and at least you get a nice bathroom. If it means sleeping, sleep. If it means wearing your loved one's clothes, do it. No one else has the answer.

"Be gentle with yourself and do what you need to do to get through."

Managing the Moment

In shock, tidal waves threatened at every turn, especially with the cataclysmic or unexpected deaths. Routine things, previously put on automatic mode seemed like gargantuan, meaningless tasks. This made the future unimaginable. I survived, at first, in ten minute snatches. I couldn't see further ahead. The minutes passed. Minutes became weeks and I could number them: *two and a half weeks now, five weeks tomorrow*. I knew deep inside if I had managed the first five weeks I could survive the next five.

"You will feel better. Focus on the moment. That's all you need to manage."

Nurturing

Managing grief is exhausting. We need to vigilantly look after ourselves and replace the energy that continually leaks away. The body, mind, and spirit must be nourished. At first, eating and drinking was too much hassle, despite wonderful friends delivering meals to me. I found though that eating told my body it was still working. Tea earned its mythical status providing fluid and pause.

I knew I was recovering four weeks after my husband's death when I found myself in running gear circuiting the local park with my dog. I focused on my breathing and the sound of my feet hitting the path and thought, 'I am alive.'

It made me cry but I knew I would be OK.

"Don't worry if you can't eat much. Eat something. Have a bath and a massage; meditate for even a few minutes; do some yoga; get out in the fresh air for a walk or a run."

Setbacks

Some days I felt I was going backwards. A birthday, anniversary, or celebration would bring a week of storm clouds or a tornado on the day. In the supermarket I often grabbed what used to be the favorite grocery of the lost person, and realized, as the grocery hit the basket like a grenade, that they didn't need it anymore.

Tears blurred the traffic as *that song* came on the car radio. Out of habit I picked up the phone to ask what they wanted for dinner. The car door banged; I thought they were home. These innocuous things, laden with meaning, were small but powerful reminders of the loss.

"Setbacks are natural, as habits and traditions take a while to digest the news. With time, we develop the gentle skill of recognizing the past, acknowledging absence and celebrating what we have."

Losing a Partner

At home for the wake, an hour after my husband's funeral, a friend leant in conspiratorially. "You're lovely. You'll find someone else."

I stood mute. *Did I hear that right?*

I imagined standing up, numbered ticket in hand, yelling, "Next!" I was stunned by the audacity and stupidity. Later I was startled by how often I heard it. Another acquaintance said, "You're lucky. At least he didn't walk out on you."

Then the dreaded financial questions followed: "Will you need to sell the house?"

These incredible conversations happened, part of the peculiar territory of the new widow(er). Where once there was a pair, now there's only one. This tearing asunder causes great unease for people around us whose faux pas attempt to reassure us and allay fears of being alone.

Those fears were real. My partner had gone. His clothes hung in the wardrobe, stark and lifeless. His side of the bed was a huge, cold reminder. Everywhere, memories, smells, and even half-finished jobs assaulted the senses. With two young teenagers, there was also a bigger load of grief to manage. But my children's needs were blessings in disguise; they helped drag me out of bed to make breakfast. They provided a focus for the immediate future; to help them recover. Their love, even crushed, was a warm shawl round my shoulders.

"Gratitude for what you have and strong intention help manage fear of the future. What you do for the children you also do for yourself."

Hope

Time does help. I do feel better. In the early days it was hard to believe that this would happen. It did. As time passed, she softened the world, and she softened me. The losses remain, always, but they are easier to carry.

On the spur of the moment, eight months after my husband died, I went to South America, danced tango in Buenos Aires, and hiked the Andes. Later, my girls went on to finish high school, go to university, and fall in love. We traveled through Italy together. Five years on, I left work to follow my passion for helping others through writing, sailed around Croatia, and fell in love.

Time heals.

Anything can happen.

About the Author

Annette Chennell is a writer who is passionate about inspiring and motivating others to transform. She has published motivational articles in health magazines and newsletters about her own remarkable journey, developed inspiring approaches to cultural transformation for major organizations, and is finalizing several manuscripts for publication concerned with physical, emotional, and spiritual transformation.

She has post-graduate degrees in science and public health and has given papers at national and international conferences. She also lectured at university and conducted educational seminars for people from all walks of life. She is now a sought-after public speaker.

Annette is the founder and director of Aria Consulting, a company concerned with change and growth, which she has run for fourteen years. Her motto "Imagine" summarizes her passion and approach to mentoring and inspiring others; inspiration, meaning, achievement, growth, in harmony, new beginnings and enrichment.

Annette has two beautiful daughters and lives in Sydney.

http://www.annettechennell.com

AWAKENING FROM THE DEPTHS WITHIN

Donna Jacques Temm

What do I believe?

I believe in the resilience of life. Even in the face of overwhelming circumstances and what appears to be impending doom.

I believe we are never on our own; that we always have access to support if we choose to receive it.

In order to anchor such beliefs in our daily living, I believe not only must we be aware and open to noticing signs and synchronicities, but we must also be willing to practice gratitude for even the smallest of blessings.

I believe that wisdom comes from life lessons brought about by both uplifting and devastating experiences.

Finally, I believe that there can be peace in *not knowing* all the answers.

I find myself in awe of even the most simplistic signs of resilience. Walking along the sidewalk in a busy, bustling city whose inhabitants are caught up in the hustle of every day responsibilities, I find a perfect example of sheer will to survive. There, growing upward toward the warmth of the sun's rays, mostly blocked by tall buildings, is a single flowering plant growing in the crack of the sidewalk's concrete. Mysteriously placed there, untended to, and not nurtured by any human contact or attention, this seed, blossoming despite adverse surroundings, is nature's sign that there exists something beyond what we're able to perceive through our five senses.

I am reminded of the power of even the smallest, random act of kindness when I think about the story I was recently told of a man who committed suicide. After jumping from the bridge to his death below, the man's body was retrieved. In searching for some form of identification, a note was found in his pocket with the short yet heart-wrenching message it contained: "I will not jump if one person smiles at me."

How resilient are humans if the contingency of life is placed upon one act of kindness by the smile of another?

Then I think of myself who, at age fourteen, had decided that life was not worth living.

Having endured ten years of sexual abuse by a non-blood relative, every ounce of my will to survive appeared to be null and void. Due to a near-death experience at the hands of the abuser, my eyes were opened to the wonderment of the spirit realm complete with its beauty, freedom, and peaceful grace. I was given a glimpse into a realm that felt like *home* minus the struggles, fear, and pain of what had been my reality for more years of my life than not.

After returning to my body to resume life in the human realm, my unwelcomed healing work was one of great distress; I carried with me anger, depression, and fear. At one point – years later – while in the midst of another crisis in my healing, I was faced with making a decision to sink or swim.

I chose to sink.

However, something much greater than myself, both within and outside of me, had a different plan. For years, I fought the healing being offered. And in choosing to go against the flow I was met with obstacle after obstacle.

This continued until I was too tired to fight or care.

Though self-imposed, I'd been solitarily riddled with this secret of abuse until well into my thirties. It was a secret I'd not only kept from others, but also from my conscious self.

Now due to the surfacing of repressed memories, the heaviness of life I recognized all-too-well returned. I had made a choice to return to this realm many years ago because of my connection with my family. Now, I found myself choosing to stay on this earth plane because of the most precious gift I've ever received during my human existence: my son.

So with the help of a professional counselor, I found myself sharing out loud what had only been silent despair and hope in its untruth.

Despite the onslaught of these memories that, once again, threatened my sense of well being, I made the choice this time to be an active part of my healing and, with help, developed coping strategies and tools that brought forth positive results and enhanced my will to live.

It wasn't until years later, when I was on my way out of the depths of my deepest despair, that I became aware of the many unnoticed blessings that had become a part of my life while in the trenches. Despite many years of anger and fear associated with PTSD (Post Traumatic Stress Disorder), I was now learning to thrive (after first choosing to do so) and was able to recognize and be grateful for the blessings in my life. It seemed as though the more gratitude I expressed, the more awareness I gained of such blessings.

Another of my strong beliefs is that well-being neither happens by accident nor is it just the luck of the draw. It is achieved by making a conscious choice and then following through with dedication to what can be very vulnerable, grueling work with a slow *two steps-forward-one-step-back* type of progress. However, my experience tells me that once you decide to live your life according to your inner authentic self, and stop living your life according to societal or familial demands or modes of acceptance, life will begin to unfold in ways you could never have imagined.

Was it an easy overnight success?

No. *Absolutely not.* But it was some of the most satisfying healing I'd experienced up to that point. Once the constant conflict and hard work necessary to break through was completed, I found I was pleased with the end result because it represented something I desired and not something that merely allowed for the comfort of others.

I vividly remember the day that I began the journey to authentically live my life, not long after I'd made the conscious decision to live. Literally. I had an emergency half-hour session with my counselor because of concern that I was dipping into the depths of despair once again. As I sat in absolute misery crying in her office and barely able to contain myself, I blubbered out the fact that I was now aware that the last thread of what I'd held as truth in my life was anything but.

At that moment, everything around me seemed to stop as my counselor spoke her next words: she stated what great news it was that what I held as truth had collapsed. Now, all the pieces of my life's puzzle were finally scattered around me and it would be our work together to pick up each piece. Then, we would decide whether those pieces had been in my life's puzzle because it was something I'd chosen, based on a belief I currently held for reasons of habit, or if it was there because it was someone else's beliefs and/or necessities that I was allowing to take priority over my own.

She went on to say that when the process was finished and the last puzzle piece was put into place, this puzzle would more accurately reflect *me*, who I am, and what I value.

What a gift that was!

It was then that I truly became empowered to be the facilitator of my own life. From that point on, my facilitation allowed me to support others, instead of allowing others to facilitate my life while I played the supporting role.

What followed was not what one would consider an easy task. Ironically, the end results were more rewarding, but the process, a daunting one.

First I had to reacquaint myself… with *myself*. I had to figure out what my true likes and dislikes were, what raised my vibration, and what lowered it. I needed to learn who I truly was for the first time ever. Then, in order to remain true to myself, I needed to make decisions based on that knowledge.

This is where the process became a bit tricky.

My decisions *now* didn't always reflect those I'd made in the *past*. As a result of my healing from within and the releasing of internalized triggers, my outward responses changed dramatically (from reactive to proactive). For those who knew and loved me, an inability to find comfort in what once had defined my predictability was experienced. This often created fear and misunderstandings for them. Though a difficult process, I was now prospering by allowing myself to be the authentic *me* I'd abandoned years before.

Despite being uncomfortable with conflict, conflict was exactly what I needed to address.

As time went on, I began looking for love, lessons, and light in every adverse experience with which I was faced. I also began to take people's less-than-desirable actions toward me less personally by becoming aware of their own wounded nature. Now I looked for the true catalyst behind their actions and, in this way, I was more easily able to simply live my life for me without long-lasting anger, resentment, or bitterness toward them. I'm not saying there wasn't hurt and heartache involved nor am I saying that I allowed my deeper understanding to enable such behavior. Instead, it allowed me to set appropriate boundaries without the necessity to completely eliminate from my life those who were important to me.

However, I also needed to use the same process of looking beyond my own outward behaviors to the catalyst within myself. I needed to see what was within me that was attracting and creating a mirroring effect. In time, I became more comfortable, and even pleased, with this new way of living life. Within a short period of time, I made three major life changes, two of which included my marital status and career path. Though the road was rough, and at times continues to be, it was all well worth it.

In order to navigate my world in the way I want to continue to do so, I often rely on my heightened spirituality.

Since finally allowing myself to own my gift of communication with the spirit world, after years of being in denial about, and then creating secrecy around it, my life has begun to prosper in a whole new way. My choice to leave the world of education as a public school elementary teacher to become an alternative therapist with a concentration on energy healing methods has been a rewarding one. It was one that has, in a sense, brought me full circle back to my authentic self. I work with many children as well as adults in my private practice.

My work has also opened me up to continue to develop my intuition, allowing me to relay to clients healing messages from loved ones who have access to a level of knowledge in the purest of form.

Looking back, which I only do on rare occasions and when it can bring healing to the now, I see how the deepest, darkest experiences of my deepest, darkest days have been some of the most influential forces in the incredible transformation of that which I now finally, with pleasure, call (and accept as) my life.

About the Author

From public education to the realm of alternative therapies, Donna is a self-employed entrepreneur whose private practice offers a myriad of noninvasive, natural therapeutic avenues empowering clients to be active forces in their own health. Through facilitation, she educates clients in recognizing self-imposed blocks to well being. She then teaches them how best to employ their gifts of intuition to reach a desired level of health and well-being.

Working with only the highest and purest vibrations of healing intentions, love, and light, Donna's intuitive ability to *see beyond the visible* and *know beyond the tangible* plays a role in client sessions at her two Maine-based locations and during remote sessions via phone with clients dispersed throughout the United States.

Donna is the author of *You're Only As Sick As Your Secrets: Sexual Abuse Awareness, Prevention, and Intervention.*

http://www.donnatemm.com

SOUL SHIFTING

Christopher Stillar

In 1996 when I was an obese twenty-nine year-old, tipping the scales at two hundred and sixty plus pounds, my life was unhappy and unfulfilled. I was literally just a shell of a man, albeit a very big one. These circumstances along with the sudden death of my dear grandmother all converged like a perfect storm forcing major life changes upon me. My life would never be the same again.

My soul was beginning its shift.

While wrapped in self-misery, grief, and despair, a tiny spark of inner light somewhere from my soul emerged. An uncharted path into a world I wasn't even sure I believed in beckoned. I just embraced the process of self-discovery knowing it was the right thing for me to do.

Almost overnight, I started to shift. Along with prayer, meditation, and a thirst for spiritual knowledge, came a new understanding that I was now ready to take control of my life. The changes were swift and apparent to those close to me. What was not obvious to the outside world was my new found awareness that I could now receive conscious communication from the spirit world: I was becoming a medium. As the famous movie punch-line goes: *I see dead people*!

I can still transport myself back to those early days reliving the moments of incredible truth and feeling the excitement of this new found wonderment. As cliché as it might sound, it was in every way a rebirthing.

My incredible need to help others had always been a steadfast component of my personality. As a teenager, I thought perhaps I would become a doctor or surgeon. But when a lack of discipline and scholastic focus reared their heads, I realized another road to service awaited me.

I honestly believe impacting another person's life in a profound and positive way makes life worth living. I am blessed to do this on a daily basis. Providing total strangers with hope, validation, the beginnings of peace, and, for many, a new truth of eternal life after a loved one's passing is life-changing to say the least.

Quite often when I first meet clients, they are at the lowest point of their life. Just like myself so many years earlier, they too are just a shell of their former selves going through a soul-shift. To witness the change in a person from the moment they walk in my office door to the time they leave is incredible. I can't put into words what that transformation is, suffice it to say the change runs deep and is profound in nature for those who have experienced a loved one's death.

My ability to see, hear, and feel those in spirit is an ability. And just like anything in life that is exercised repetitively, my connection with those in spirit gets stronger and more defined. I believe that we all possess the ability to communicate with departed loved ones, and so I make it my mission in life to empower people to facilitate their own personal connection with loved ones in spirit. All of us continue to have a relationship with our deceased loved ones. Whether it is a conscious relationship with those in spirit or an unconscious one is entirely up to each of us.

Recently as I was lecturing to a small crowd of a couple hundred people, the clock was winding down, and two hours after being on stage, I was almost done. Suddenly, without warning, I was pulled to the right side of the theater to a young lady sitting in the third row. A young girl in spirit who had passed from cancer came through to her. Caught off guard, and not sure I was even with her, Melissa (I later found out her name) was reluctant to acknowledge the presence of the spirit.

The little girl's persistence won out until she was recognized by Melissa. This young girl was a close friend of Melissa's family who passed a couple years before. As amazed as Melissa was over her visitor, the spirit world held more surprises for her that evening. The little girl brought forth an older gentleman with her who stood next to Melissa's seat. Emotions were running at a fever pitch by this point and Melissa's grief poured out of her upon hearing me say I felt a connection coming through, sensing the letters J.O. She was sobbing as she asked if it could be John.

I replied that it most definitely was.

Visibly shaking, she said, "That's my father."

My next words also caught her off guard when I asked if she understood why I was getting a suicide connection within her immediate family. She looked up and spoke softly into the microphone saying, "We were never sure," before her voice trailed off. She cleared her throat and said, "The police could not rule either way. It was inconclusive."

I looked at her and said, "Your father wants you to know he is so sorry for what he did. But please know he is safe and remains with you throughout your life."

Melissa contacted me days after the show and I asked her to share her story. Following is her account of it:

When I got the phone call in late March from my mom that my dad had died, I was completely devastated. It was so unexpected. I felt as though the only person in the world who completely understood me was gone.

Dad had diabetes and had difficulty controlling his blood sugar. On face value, it looked as though his blood sugar had gotten too high, and he overcompensated with his fast-acting insulin. The coroner's report said that his cause of death was a heart attack. Unfortunately, there were some things that just didn't add up for us and it weighed heavily in our hearts that perhaps this hadn't been an accident at all.

I dwelled on the uncertainty of his last moments. He had been in the hospital so many times in the past, I had always thought that I would have the chance to be there with him when he passed. When the time came, he was alone. I wondered if he had not seen it coming; if it had all been a mistake. Was his soul in limbo? Or was someone there for him, someone to help him cross over? Only my dad knew and although I thought of him every day I felt like I could never really be sure of the answers.

When I was alone I would talk to him but the frustration of not hearing him and not feeling him usually left me in tears.

My friend, told me about an opportunity to go and see a medium named Chris Stillar. She told me that he'd helped a number of families in the community and that it was obvious to her that my father's passing was still affecting me. I'll admit I was a bit skeptical but the date of the show gave me goose bumps. It was the day before the one year anniversary of my father's passing. I told her that I didn't know if my dad would go for that sort of thing or not and she just suggested that I talk with my dad about it.

Chris seemed to be the genuine article. If I accepted that he could possibly make contact with my dad, I needed to be prepared for it.

I told Dad that there was a gentleman that was doing a show on Saturday and that he could hear him. I let him know that I had forgiven him for whatever had happened... whether it had been intentional or accidental. I was worried that he might be in limbo, if it had been sudden and unexpected. I needed to know that he wasn't alone when he died. Had someone been there to help him cross over? I trusted that if he felt it was right to answer these questions, he would. I talked to him every day leading up to Chris' show.

The day came and when Chris came out on the stage, I had to smile thinking, "That's the guy I've been telling you about, Dad. Talk to him and he'll let me know."

Chris started passing messages on to people in the audience. I just listened quietly and focused on hearing from my dad. Message after message was put forth to the audience. When it seemed like things were wrapping up, I got a bit anxious. I thought, "Dad, this could be your last chance to talk with me. Please, if there's anything that you need to say to me, come to Chris and he'll pass the message on to me."

Chris started to get a message from a young girl who had died from cancer and he was indicating it came from our area. My husband nudged me reminding me of a girl who had been very close to my dad. When she had died, Dad told me it was as though he had lost his own daughter. We were whispering back and forth and Chris noticed. I didn't want to just make it fit and he asked me if what he was saying made sense to me. I told him that yes we had known a girl that died of cancer just after graduating high school. He asked if her mother had an illness. I told him that yes, she did. Understandably, he wasn't entirely sure if the message was for me or not and neither was I.

Chris started to get a man's name and when he got the first two letters out, I knew this message was for me. When I said my father's name, Chris seemed certain that the message was for me.

He told me that the young girl was like a daughter (but not) and that she had been there to help my dad cross over. I tried to hold back the tears but couldn't. He told me that he had something important to tell me because I had questions. "Suicide," he said. I managed to say that we were not sure. He told me that it had been and that my father had put a lot of thought into it because he didn't want to smear the family. He told me that my father took responsibility for it and that he didn't want me to blame myself. He told me that my father wanted me to know that he was okay and that he was not in limbo. He stated that he was sorry and he wanted me to know that he is always with me and that he loves me very much.

I sat there trying to understand what exactly I was crying about. Certainly I was sad but it was more than that. It was mostly the shock of validation; suddenly knowing that my father could still hear me and was still looking out for me. Without even knowing it, Chris managed to answer every one of the questions I had been asking my father.

I feel that the information I was given has made it possible for me to move forward in the healing process. I don't have to dwell on the uncertainty anymore. This experience has taught me the importance of shifting my perception: if I could communicate with my dad in the hereafter then there really is no limit to what the Law of Attraction can manifest for me.

Melissa's story demonstrates how her power of belief, trust, and openness for something she could not see or hear led her to a place of healing and understanding. Her beloved father found a way to get his message through to her and by doing so, helped facilitate the first steps in her road to healing. Melissa's father was only one part of the equation; Melissa herself had to remain open to the possibility of spirit communication in order for her father to be successful in his attempts of having his messages heard.

Melissa's story is not unique to me; I am blessed to play a part in real-life stories like hers each and every day. You too can find healing and peace of mind with your loved one's passing, if you believe and trust that the bonds of love and connection remain strong following physical death.

I have learned in my sixteen years of doing this work that our loved ones in spirit are around us, standing next to us, loving us, feeling our every emotion, and hearing our every thought. To many, this may sound too good to be true or perhaps even a fairytale. I promise you it's not.

There is no distance or space that love can't transcend, even through the immeasurable pain of physical death.

As a medium, I have achieved many milestones and accolades during my career. The recognition I have received and the notoriety that has been placed on me because of my work are nice, but they do not feed my soul. The true reward for me and the only thing that fills my soul and brings me joy beyond measure is when I help others realize their own potential. I'm being daily blessed to watch people just like Melissa find healing and hope as they undergo their very own soul-shift.

About the Author

Christopher Stillar has been a professional medium since 1996. He is the author of the newly released book, Pennies from Heaven and is the only medium to be endorsed and trusted to work with MADD Canada and the families victimized by impaired driving. His clients are worldwide, some from as far away as Africa, Holland, the continental United States and Canada. Through his life-changing ability of spirit communication and public speaking engagements, Chris has touched thousands of lives. He has appeared on television, radio and been featured in countless print media publications.

http://www.spiritualmedium.ca

BECOMING VISIBLE: MY HEALING JOURNEY

Lynne Thorsen

My journey into metaphysical belief and spirituality began in 1999 after my then-boyfriend left me unexpectedly, and I experienced my first *emotional crisis*. This story reveals how I healed myself from within and truly became *visible* from the inside out. As a result, I had changed my world.

Previously I had never released the tightly-held grip on my emotions and, for the first time, I found myself reeling out of control. I delved into the esoteric, found a mentor, and explored many areas of metaphysical and spiritual beliefs. However, before I could achieve true enlightenment, I left this path for the security of normality. I got married and had three beautiful children.

My life was fun and interesting and all-consuming. We spent four years in London, and then spent seven years travelling back and forth between my native Australia and our farmhouse in France. Outwardly, life was great; inwardly, I was experiencing increasing levels of personal conflict.

When we moved to France permanently in 2009, I experienced another deep existential crisis, which spelled out: "Who am I? Why am I here?"

I understood that coming to France had just been another excuse to escape from myself. What I hadn't bargained on was that once here, there was nowhere to hide and nowhere to run. I really didn't have any idea how to make it better. I felt like a failure because, in my mind, my three most significant relationships – my husband's, my daughter's, and my mother's – were full of unresolved conflict and emotion.

Little did I realize at the time that it was the relationship with myself that required the most attention.

I finally confessed my misery to my husband. His loving support gave me hope and I started searching online for something meaningful to do. My search led me to England and Binnie A. Dansby's courses in SOURCE Process & Breathwork.

Though I didn't know it then, I had found my lifeline.

In August 2010, I joined SOURCE's training course in Estonia and started an amazing journey of healing. This system of breathwork was giving me a tool to begin healing some very deep and painful wounds. Before long, during my second seminar, I decided I wanted to become a writer. I realized that before writing about anything else, I needed to write my own story. I had wanted to write it for many years and thought I couldn't because it was not something I could or would share with anyone.

Over the years, *My Story* had become lost in a tangled web of incomplete versions, deliberate distortions, and suppressed memories. I felt an incredible desire to express what had previously been suppressed!

Firstly, writing allowed me to explore and connect previously separated parts of the sum of my life's experience. I discovered that childhood decisions and conditioning had led me to believe I was an outsider in my own family, influencing my choices as I progressed into adolescence. The choices I made had led to painful decisions about myself, my place in the world, and a further separation of the parts.

As I veered between sexual abuse, eating disorders and dysfunctional relationships, I became very adept at burying my deepest hurts. I locked my most negative thoughts in a dark vault away from others and, more importantly, from myself. I believed I was alone, and I therefore couldn't open myself to the support that was always around me both physically and spiritually. As I emerged into young adulthood, I began discovering I could make some empowering decisions. However, my innocent child was locked deep in that same dark vault; her awareness separated from the adult. Unable to see the truth and powerless to move forward, this created a conflict in me that I couldn't resolve.

Secondly, the revelations and connections to myself gave me the courage to share this very honest account with significant people from my past and present. The sharing of *My Story* ensured my visibility, reinforced my love for myself, and opened me to experience unconditional support from my friends. I began to share *My Story* over the following twelve months. I discovered that each person resonated with a different part of the story. *My Story* was creating healing for others too.

At around this time, I suffered a devastatingly painful knee-injury. "Why me? Why now?" I thought to myself. Examining my previous knee-injuries from a metaphysical perspective, I had concluded that both of them had occurred at pivotal times in my life where I had made life-diminishing decisions. The first knee-injury had occurred when I was just sixteen and the second when I was twenty-eight. So why was this happening now, when I was becoming so content with myself?

My visit to the surgeon confirmed my worst fears. My left knee required another complete knee reconstruction. Old feelings of failure and unworthiness emerged within me. Fortunately enough, I had enlightened support around me and I realized that I was being presented with an opportunity to heal myself.

I started to use conscious breathing and visualization techniques to create healing. I called on the Healing Masters of the Universe to help me. I did this nearly everyday for three weeks and then I attended the next breathwork seminar, which was the SOURCE Warm Water Event. It was my first conscious breathing experience while immersed in warm water, and I was blown away by the healing energy that filled the space in the tub room. I completely immersed myself in the whole process and found that supporting others was even more inspiring than my own session.

The day after I returned from the seminar, I had to undergo an MRI, ordered by my surgeon. Afterwards, the radiologist seemed perplexed and questioned me as to the current state of my knee. I was still using crutches and wearing a brace, although, during the seminar, I had found that I could walk more and more without the aid of the crutches. I was very surprised when I read the radiologist's report, which indicated that he could find no evidence of a ruptured anterior cruciate ligament. I went to the surgeon the next day and after reading the report and examining my knee, he declared I no longer required a knee reconstruction.

I was in a state of disbelief, followed by a state of joy and then a state of fear.

The doubting voice in my head appeared: what if your knee doesn't heal properly on its own? After some weeks, my knee had almost regained full function; I couldn't extend it fully however, and still had a nagging pain. I think this was my last piece of resistance of self-healing so, instead of going deeper within, I convinced myself and everyone else that I needed minor surgery to repair the damaged cartilage.

At this point, I fell back into old patterns of behavior and negative thinking. I contracted and stopped sharing *My Story*. Fortunately, after three months, my breathwork course resumed. During the following seminar, I experienced a very powerful healing process with regards to my relationship with my mother. I realized that all the negative thoughts I had about our relationship were of my own creation. The *she did it to me* notion turned into an *I am doing it to her* one. I was blocking our relationship on every level and blaming her for it.

Wow, that was a body blow! However this realization totally changed my perception and I started to live my life from a much more authentic place.

The next topic was about *manifestation*. For many years I had intellectually agreed with the principles of both manifesting and self-healing and I could do both to a point. However, during that weekend, more pieces of the puzzle fell into place and I embodied several key concepts:

1. I can heal myself.

2. Giving and receiving are the same.

3. Manifestation required focused intention and persistent action.

4. Seeing is not believing; believing is seeing.

I shared *My Story* with a number of new people and enjoyed deeply connected relationships as a result. I connected with my own innocence and this created healing with and for my ten year-old daughter. I felt like I was on the fast track. Every seminar seemed to go straight to the heart of the issue that was on top, matching perfectly to create the ultimate healing experience.

When the student is ready, the teacher appears!

The writing and sharing of *My Story* had made me visible and opened me up to the love and support that had always been there. I had created significant healing in all my key relationships such as that of my husband, mother, daughter, and friends.

So what next?

What came next was unexpected. The topic of the seminar was *change* and I thought, "Great, I love change!" We explored our own births as our Source experience of change. What I discovered was that I had always used change to escape fears, keep separated and avoid success. It was my defining pattern.

All my life, I had capped my achievement at around the A-standard 80-85% mark. However, this was still far from perfection, so whenever I achieved this level of success, I would engineer the idea of *change* so I would have to start again. I took on the mantra, *Jack of all trades, Master of none*. It is this glass ceiling of my own creation that I had been hitting up against on this journey of healing. I hadn't understood why I had still failed to manifest greater success, as I didn't *see* or *perceive* that this imaginary glass ceiling was there. I now also understood *why* I created it.

The Source experience for it was my *birth*.

My birth was a success of my own creation; I was in charge and it was a triumph; an easy birth with little trauma to mother or child. I entered the world in a state of joy only to discover that no one was acknowledging my role and my success. They didn't welcome me as the hero!

My next SOURCE breathwork session was amazing. I left *ego consciousness* behind and connected with *Universal consciousness*. My physical body melted away and I became one with the golden light. I experienced the purest state of peace and joy that I had ever known. I knew that I could achieve whatever I wanted to do. I had had the ability all along to completely heal my knee and even avoid the minor surgery. My knee was still not completely healed, and I knew that it was within my power to change that.

As the weeks passed, I started to experience resistance at what felt like a cellular level, and my knee still hurt. We continued to explore change, and I uncovered a core operating belief. I realized that I had also stepped into a widely held societal belief; one that creates much ugliness and suffering in the world. I had previously believed that I needed to judge everyone from the basis of *I am better than you* or *you are better than me*. And because I was unable to see the goodness and equality that is everyone's essence of being, this created an internal conflict whereby I would feel guilty and limit my achievements, or I would feel the desperate need to prove my worth and subsequently underperform due to anxiety levels. This impeded my levels of success and thwarted my attempts at happiness.

Through a process of forgiveness, I had a paradigm shift.

Within two days, my knee healed completely. I resumed running and playing basketball. In addition, the writing and publishing of this story became my first step to achieving my goal of becoming a successful writer.

I Am Visible.

I Am Whole.

We are all Spirit manifest in beautiful form.

About the Author

Lynne Thorsen is a qualified holistic therapist in integrated self-empowerment therapy (ISET) and is currently completing her training in SOURCE therapeutic breathwork in Estonia. Previously, she enjoyed a diverse set of careers in physical education, hospitality management and travel.

Lynne was born in Melbourne and now lives in southwest France with her husband and three children.

She has lived abroad in the UK, France and the USA, traveled extensively all over the world and still calls Australia home!

Lynne's great passion and purpose is the Revolution of Birth Consciousness and she is working on several projects to increase awareness in this area, including her first book, a website/blog and an empowering birth program. Her three children were all born at home in three different countries, UK, Australia and France.

http://www.lynnethorsen.com

HEALING THE ILLUSION

Caroline Cory

It is commonly said that, as a human, you must hit rock bottom in order to have an epiphany or to understand the true meaning of things. There seems to be an agreement that our physical body must break down and deteriorate, and it is the journey to recovery that will open the doorways to our enlightenment. And so you hear of many survival stories such as those who face and surmount the darkest side of life-threatening illnesses.

You cannot help but feel compelled to encourage and support those who have suffered through these dreadful physical and emotional pains. I too feel much compassion and praise towards these remarkable individuals. However, along with those feelings, also comes much confusion on the matter. Why is it that humans must first suffer in order to attain freedom or joy? Why is it that we must first embrace our shadow side, as some like to call it, in order to find truth and higher wisdom? I am one of those who believe that human nature is not meant to suffer. In fact, I truly do not agree with the philosophies that support pain as the way to reach spiritual enlightenment. My findings are based on my own journey and a series of experiences I would call *reaching the highest high*, as opposed to hitting rock bottom.

Let me explain.

It happened many years ago on a hot and breezy day in Florida. I was sitting quietly on my porch, appreciating the silence and beauty of nature, when I noticed that the red ant stings I had gotten on the beach earlier that afternoon had swollen and formed a huge bulge on my right thigh. As I stared at it apprehensively, I suddenly heard a voice saying, "Ask the lump to disappear. Ask the swelling to stop and disappear."

Without questioning the reason or origin of the voice, I asked the now very painful and malicious-looking bulge to go away. To my astonishment, it began to shrink and within seconds, it vanished completely before my eyes!

I was terrified. I ran inside and hid in the bedroom trying to contain my emotions and pounding heart. *What had I done and how could that be? Is it possible to simply ask and make such things happen instantaneously?* I was baffled and disturbed to say the least but quickly managed to dismiss the incident as a ploy of my own mind and imagination.

The next day, I watched my friend lay in pain from a lower back injury when the voice once more spoke: "Ask to relieve his pain. All you have to do is *ask.*"

Curious about these odd happenings, I decided to attempt helping him somehow. I began placing my hand on his lower back area when he suddenly shrieked. "Stop! You are burning me!"

His reaction startled me and as I stared incomprehensibly at the palm of my hand, I wondered, "How could I burn him when my hand is still four or five inches away from his body? Within seconds though, his pain had vanished.

My daily healing miracles ranged from relieving pain to manifesting situations almost instantaneously. They continued on relentlessly without any summoning on my part. In fact, it is the very fact that such experiences occurred so effortlessly that confused me at the time.

As a *normal* human would do, I began looking for explanations and answers in articles, books, the internet, and everywhere else I could think of. I eventually was able to dismiss the possibility that these happenings were the product of my own imagination or that I may be suffering from some brain imbalance of some sort. I also knew that the voice was nothing but my own higher mind and guidance system that had become so clear as to be heard as a distinct voice. So could I have mysteriously stumbled upon some other-worldly healing method? *Could I heal others as well as I did myself?* The questions continued.

With time, I realized that the more I searched for answers, the more I became aware that my *asking* or my thought had created my experience. In fact, that was precisely what the voice had urged me to do: to *ask*, meaning to focus my intent and thought and articulate my desire accurately. I came to understand the dynamics of creating reality instantly using my own mind to ask-intend. This would apply not just for those things related to my physical state of being but for those connected to my outer reality as well. More importantly, I realized that these experiences of asking had nothing to do with healing! They had to do with *me*. They had to do with my ability to tap into *my own power to create my own reality* – which happens to include healing.

Lesson number one: Once you decide to stop looking for healing provided by a source outside yourself, then, and only then, can you truly begin creating the reality of your choosing.

Since that time of continued effortless manifestation, I associated a new meaning to the word *healing*. To me, we are not healing from an illness, an emotional imbalance, or a mental malaise. We are healing from our own illusion and belief that the intervention, the help, and the resolutions must come from an outside source. This illusion is the biggest disease! The lack of trust, the lack of belief in our own Divine nature and exquisite consciousness is indeed *the* disease.

The question remained however: How do we heal this illusion and the addiction to needing someone or something better, bigger, and more powerful than us? Following the same principle, I would say that the answer also must lie within our own being.

Back to my journey's unfolding.

I focused on the reason for my creating these experiences and realized that my experiences also reflected my beliefs. I did not believe in physical suffering as a means to enlightenment nor did I believe in daunting karmic debts that are impossible to circumvent or overcome. What I did believe in was an intimate and direct link to a Universal Source that creates and knows all things; a creator; a mind-heart-being Source that maintains the life force and original blueprint alive throughout creation and all life forms in existence – and that included me in physical form.

Somehow, I believed that all I had to do was to maintain and focus on this Universal flow of Source through me and all would be well. I reached for the understanding of this Universal flow and found many avenues to retrieve and comprehend this Source of infinite possibilities. However, as I began searching for evidence of its existence right here on Earth, I suddenly became terribly disillusioned and highly discouraged. I thought to myself that if I was incapable of finding this Source of life on Earth then others must inevitably feel the same.

I struggled with that thought for a while until I reached an understanding that became the turning point in my earthly career. This understanding is based on the principle that all existence is a form of energy, meaning that the physical body, as well as our emotions, thoughts, and everything else in between, is a form of energy holding an inherent vibrational pattern. This vibrational pattern can be coherent or incoherent with others' vibrational patterns. Imbalance occurs when two energy forms are vibrationally incoherent. We, as energy beings in physical form, are meant to be in vibrational coherence with the Universal Source, which in turn, will maintain our physical apparatus and human consciousness in alignment with our higher mind and spiritual guidance system.

This alignment with the Universal Source permits an effortless realization and manifestation as in the case of my instant healings. Instead, we occupy our daily human lives with objects and experiences that are incoherent with the Universal vibrational patterns. These objects and experiences include individuals and situations to which we hold on, out of need, incompetence, scarcity, or simply out of fear of being alone.

In time, this vibrational mismatch changes the original pattern of our physical cells, our mind channels, and our emotional state – which we then call "imbalance" and even disease. The imbalance or disease is in fact nothing but a drop in our cells' vibrational frequency to a range between 150 to 350Hz on average. The answer is then to raise once more that frequency to its original pattern and restore the original vibrational match of our physical being with the life force of the Universe, the Universal Source. The process of raising our vibration will instantly reestablish the natural pattern of effortless being and creating.

The scope of this chapter does not allow me to expand on the many intricate technical details on which I have based such crucial findings. However, the many years of practicing and applying such principles provided, many times over, consistent evidence and definite sustained positive results. In this publication, I will therefore simply share the way by which you could restore vibrational balance with the Universal Source instantly and, by doing so, your physical cells will spontaneously raise their frequency between 734Hz and 1,000Hz. This vibrational range is what the Universal Source comprehends and associates with, and through which it can maintain its coherence with your being on Earth.

Here are seven simple steps to attain a universally coherent vibration:

1. Breathe in deeply through the nose and out through the mouth.

2. Begin to invoke Source through your own asking-and-intending.

3. Intend to purify your instrument and realign with the Universal Source.

4. Intend to raise your vibration between 734Hz and 1,000Hz.

5. Imagine Source light coming through your being purifying each cell within your body and restoring its vibrational balance.

6. Breathe in deeply through the nose and out through the mouth again.

7. Relax, enjoy and notice how you feel.

We are at a pivotal time on Earth when these higher vibrations are more present and available such as in the above explanations and principles. I believe we have come to a crossroad at which humanity is ready to take a turn and shift into a new reality that is in vibrational alignment with higher truths and spiritual wisdom. However, this change and tremendous task begins with you. You must first believe that your place on the earth is purposeful and your presence is required for the shifting of the human collective consciousness into a higher vibration that is coherent with Source. In fact, your presence on Earth contributes greatly to the expansion of the planetary and galactic consciousness, and by extension, will push the Universe into an entirely new configuration.

You are endowed, as are all humans, with the ability to think and ask, therefore to create, and each one of your creations on Earth propels a reciprocal creation on a universal level. Think about it: Your human thought and asking add information and contribute to the greater good of the Universe!

So you can now make a choice to begin healing your physicality and your addiction to being inadequate and even your perception of being *the lesser* intelligent life form in the Universe. In other words, ask to heal the human illusion and your most profound and complete healing will begin within you.

About the Author

Caroline Cory is a futurist, a visionary, and the founder of the Omnium Experiential Method of Learning and Healing. She is the creator of the New Paradigm Education System and the Connecting To Source meditation technique. She teaches an international audience from ninety-two countries through tele-classes, webinars, and live events such topics as: mind mastery, spiritual awakening and self-realization, DNA reconfiguration, zero point, time suspension, and more.

Caroline's experience with the worlds of consciousness, energy medicine and spirituality started at the age of five when she began perceiving a form of subtle energy she defines as *the Source of all energy forms in existence, which spring from the center of each Universe and ultimately meet at the first center of creation: The Creator-Source.*

Caroline bases her experiential teaching on these fundamental basics and understanding. She is now creating a new learning method based on multimedia light and sound entrainment techniques.

http://www.omniumuniverse.com

SHARE YOUR STORY AND JOIN THE COMMUNITY

Have a Story to Share?

Everyone has a story, including you! With several *Adventures in Manifesting* titles in production each year, we are constantly looking for more journeys to share. Ask yourself, *what story of mine could change someone's life?*

Whether you have a story to tell or lesson to teach, we're listening. Share yours and get the guide to writing and submitting your chapter here:

www.AdventuresInManifesting.org

The stories we keep an eye out for are any that has to do with manifesting (success, spirituality, health, happiness, wealth, love prosperity, inner guidance, achieving dreams, overcoming obstacles, etc.).

If chosen as a top submission, we will get in touch directly to invite you to be a part of one of our next *Adventures in Manifesting* titles.

Looking for Guidance?

AdventuresInManifesting.org is also a place to freely join a course & community with lessons and action guides for manifesting.

By training you to develop rituals for success and creating the space to get the energy flowing, it will enable you to focus on your intentions from the purest place possible.

www.AdventuresInManifesting.org

Join now to surround yourself with some incredible individuals. It truly is a place of joyful intention marked with the loving energy of gratitude and appreciation.

Feeling Inspired?

We always love to hear how our readers were touched, inspired or changed by the stories shared. If you'd like to share your experience, then you guessed it, hop on over to the AdventuresInManifesting.org home page to let us know!

MORE ADVENTURES IN MANIFESTING TITLES

--iBooks and Kindle--

All Älska titles can be found through the www.AdventuresInMani-festing.org portal or requested from your local bookstore (and found through online bookstores as well).

<u>Books</u>

Adventures in Manifesting: Success and Spirituality

Adventures in Manifesting: Health and Happiness

Adventures in Manifesting: Passion and Purpose

Adventures in Manifesting: Healing from Within

Adventures in Manifesting: Love and Oneness

<u>The Kindle and iBooks</u>

Each of the Adventures in Manifesting titles above can also be purchased via the Amazon Kindle or iTunes iBook formats via AdventuresInManifesting.org.

SHARE WITH LOVE

Is someone you know on the deep and profound journey within? If so, be sure to share with them the entire book or specific stories you intuitively felt would resonate with them.

The meaning of Älska is 'to Love' (it's a Swedish Verb!)

The *chapters* were written with Love.

The *book* was published with Love.

And now it's up to you to *share* with Love.

From the bottom of our hearts and deepest depths of our soul, thank you, thank you, thank you.

With Love & Gratitude,

Älska

http://www.AlskaPublishing.com